Bored.

Why we need something to do every day
(and what happens if we don't)

Jen Gash

DEDICATION

To you all – may your boredom be a source of joy, love and understanding.
To the earth – may you survive all our attempts to escape our boredom.

CONTENTS

ACKNOWLEDGMENTS

Once again, my beautiful eldest daughter, Jillie, has been a tower of strength, a sounding bored (!), and a source of inspiration. She kept the faith when I couldn't.

Introduction

Books like this often start with a Chinese proverb, meaningful poem or ancient Hindu parable, but you won't find one here. Whilst I am sure there are hundreds of appropriate fables featuring wise elders, an old pot and a special tree, our modern-day struggles with boredom are so complex, and I don't feel that a weirdly worded quote from someone who lived around 400 BC would help. They lived without the joy and pain of WIFI, ready meals, unused gym memberships, Facebook, FOMO, and the never-ending scrolling through Netflix.

What I offer in this book is the result of many years of professional work in helping people "do stuff" alongside a goodly amount of personal "doing", resulting in creative outputs such as books and paintings with varying success. But, more importantly, I have included insights from a busy life trying to keep my family, and me, occupied, well-satisfied and motivated without damaging the planet and those I live with (oh, and there might be a bit of swearing here and there!).

Why me?

I have always been fascinated with boredom. As a child who struggled to engage with hobbies and clubs, I never developed an interest outside school. I struggled through the long school holidays. I wasn't one for hanging around the shopping centre, as it was boring and I hated it when my friends were noisy or disruptive. I vividly remember my father's attempts at introducing me to new hobbies. The first one revolved around teaching me to sew, well, tailor, actually.

I was about ten years old and longed to make a Day-Glo, ra-ra skirt as simply and quickly as possible. Unfortunately, my loving dad was too old-fashioned in his approach to sewing and I quickly lost interest in making the grey, woollen, lined, tailored trousers, which involved multiple stages and days upon days of concentration. I never did finish them. A few years later, a friend of my mum's succeeded where my well-intentioned dad had failed. She captured my interest in dressmaking, which became a hobby until my late twenties. The difference was simple – this time, we made something simple, fashionable, and wearable, and it only took an hour or so to complete. My short attention span was satisfied and resulted in something actually wearable!

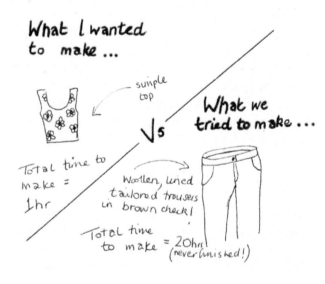

What I wanted to make ...

simple top

Vs

What we tried to make ...

Total time to make = 1hr

Woollen, lined tailored trousers in brown check!

Total time to make = 20hrs (never finished!)

Dad's second attempt to stop me moaning about being bored and develop a hobby saw him introduce me to the local amateur dramatic group. This succeeded in improving my confidence, gave me a hobby, and helped me make new friends. To this day, I still harbour a secret desire to become an actress.

Fast forward a few years, I was ready to leave school and was keen to get a job rather than face three or four years at university, which was way too long in my mind. So, after a few years and trying several positions, I trained as an occupational therapist (I'm also a coach and professional artist, but more about that later). Nope, we are not "Occupational Health" or "Occupational Psychology", and we don't just do stuff to do with work or getting a job. Occupational therapists specialise in **"doing"** – that's what the word **"occupation"** actually means. Occupational therapists believe in **the power of activity to create, restore, and heal, enabling human beings to engage and participate at home, work and in the community**, so you can see why boredom became a genuine interest to me.

As a mum and a wife, I watched my kids grow, fascinated by how differently they played and how different they were in their ability to engage in activities and concentrate. My youngest would sit for hours making Lego® and drawing, with little help to get going. On the other hand, my eldest struggled to engage, had a short attention span, preferred immediate gratification, or opted to just be with me and chat. My husband doesn't even have the word "bored" in his vocabulary – he is addicted to "doing", and even during rare downtime in front of the TV, his hands and taste buds are still kept busy by snacking. Most TV shows and films are "too slow" for him.

As a parent, I have long pondered what might be the most important things I should teach my kids or help them understand as fledgling human beings. When you see your child struggle with something so debilitating such as depression, as I have, you seek the answer to this question even more so.

"I'm happiest when I am busy, or at least knowing I have something to do each day."

My eldest daughter, at 17, emerging from severe depression.

What I know now is that after keeping our kids fed and alive, our primary jobs as parents are: 1) to help them understand their physical, mental, spiritual, social, and psychological needs and how to meet those needs without being an arse to others; 2) to understand and accept, to a certain degree, our imperfections, blind-spots and fuck-ups, whilst also embracing how adaptable, resilient, creative and resourceful we are; and 3) to understand what it means to be human, with finite existence and the choices inherent in that finite existence.

Why now?

These days, my interest in boredom and how we spend our days has grown, partly due to the impact of technology, increases in health problems, and the challenges of climate change. Many of us respond to gaps in activity, which we often label "boredom", by scrolling on our phones, snacking, or going shopping. I have started to see how people's innate need to create, "do", and experience variety has run amok, causing many of the world's problems, including over-consumption and excessive travel.

As a species, we need to understand how important it is for human "beings" to do something purposeful every day. We need to use our hands, heads, and hearts daily, but we also must embrace downtime without becoming physically or mentally ill, causing distress to others or damaging the planet. We are infinitely creative as a species, but we must use this for good.

Trust me; I'm not preaching or throwing stones inside my glass house. As a human being, I have done all sorts of things to relieve boredom. I have taken holidays because I was bored, gone shopping for something I didn't need because it was raining and I didn't know what else to do, and many other boredom-relieving activities that subsequently threatened my marriage, career, finances, and health. I am a failed eco-warrior and no angel.

The recent pandemic brought the issue of boredom to the forefront of many people's minds, as our usual daily activities were disrupted and restricted, and we had to adapt quickly. Many people lost their jobs and had their daily lives turned upside down. People had to work from home, lost social contact, or adapted to having a house full of people. We all had to find new ways to exercise and keep positive. We had to adjust our daily habits and structure in almost every aspect. Whilst lockdown also introduced new "ways" of socialising and keeping active, much of it was online, and vast parts of our community became very isolated. We are a species fuelled by social, sensory, and physical activities, and the broader impact of online parties, exercise, learning, dating, and doctors appointments will probably never be fully understood. And I don't know about you, but the pandemic seems to have opened a door for many changes that were "temporary" or "emergency measures" but are now accepted as the norm. As an aside, this is a classic tactic for societal change, and we can see this tactic used many times in history.

Before Covid, other things like Brexit, Trump, the usual political noise, and fake and "real" news were already providing a noisy distraction, taking attention away from the challenge of climate change. We have known for decades about the massive impact climate change will likely have on our human existence. No longer on the horizon but much closer to home, these "future" challenges have started to unfold and require us to "do" life differently. Aside from climate change and other environmental issues, I also think about the changing nature of work and leisure, our changing population demographics, and the impact of people living longer with complex health and social care needs. Boredom has a relationship with all of these modern challenges and impacts in all sorts of ways, which we need to understand much better.

Chapter 1 – Human Being or Human Doing?

Time and time again, I come back to the fact that our self-assigned label "human being" is hugely inaccurate. A dictionary definition of the term "being" refers to "existence", or the notion of something's soul or psyche. However, I would argue that **we are defined by what we do, say, make, or achieve** more than what we think or feel. We are **human doings**, much more than human beings. From the moment we wake, we start "doing" or planning our days "doing". By the end of our day, we might have a long list of things we have done (or, in my case, an even longer list of things still needing to be done), and usually a much smaller list accounting for the "being" side of life. If you have trouble sleeping, you probably also spend the night thinking and worrying about what you still need to do, or dreaming about what might happen if you do or don't do it all!

If I think about my future obituary, I doubt that it will include a list of achievements or accomplishments for the "being" side of my life, such as, "She existed successfully", or "Jen had some interesting thoughts in her head" or "Jen meditated well". We are remembered by what we did and how our actions made people feel, not what we merely thought about doing. Even if you are a professional thinker or philosopher, you would "do" something about it rather than keep it in your head; things like write books or articles, speak or teach, and these days, probably make videos, podcasts or TikToks.

Whilst we need to pay attention to our "being", as it's evident that our emotions, spirit and cognitions steer or drive what we do, it's our behaviours, words and actions that structure our lives, give us meaning, and define who we are. **"What do you do?"** is the most common thing said when we first meet someone, is it not?

However, our innate need to "do" comes with many pitfalls, as the most common ways to deal with "big" boredom are travel, sex, and substance misuse (Toohey, 2011). We are currently the most stressed-out, overweight, addicted, and in debt that we have ever been, and we are gobbling up the world's resources at an alarming rate. Despite literally having the world at their fingertips, our young people still complain of being bored, and at the same time they are struggling with depression, alienation, and addiction more than ever before.

Some argue that rather than boredom being due to a lack of varied activity, it is actually the opposite. It results from **too much opportunity and choice** (Martin, Sadlo & Stew 2006). Basically, we are spoilt for choice.

Our innate need to "do" needs serious consideration. Every one of us is immeasurably practical, adaptable, and creative, but we need to keep busy somehow. We need to participate in "doing" that not only provides us with meaning and purpose, but in a way that is not damaging to the environment or those around us. Our daily "doing" needs to enhance human existence, not threaten it further or result in the unhappiness of others. If you think about climate change, it is basically caused by various human "doings" yet we hear constant shouts of "it's the fault of the corporations", "ban this and, whilst you are at it, ban that", "we need new laws", "it's the government's fault", "it's the baby boomers' fault". I hear very little talk of how every one of us needs to be busy and do stuff each day, and that these activities are almost as damaging as those naughty corporations. At the very least, our boredom drives those companies, their profits, and their products we both outwardly condemn but secretly love.

I was going to call this chapter "a history of human doing", but people often skip chapters that contain the word "history". However, looking back at human evolution is helpful in understanding our need to "do" and perhaps what "boredom" might be about. There are so many great books out there that describe human evolution and how we became what we are today. I read *Sapiens* (Yuval Noah Harari, 2014) a couple of years ago, and it gave me lots of new perspectives and filled many gaps in my knowledge and understanding – it's a very worthy read, if not a rather long one.

People often say that humans are just animals who have lost their fur, and whilst there is some truth in that, we are pretty different from other animals. Let's jump to the bit where we evolved from apes, eventually standing up and starting to walk. From here, in simplistic terms, walking on two legs freed up our hands to be used in different ways and our brains to start changing – this was roughly two million years ago. We like to benchmark evolutionary changes in chunks or leaps to make them more understandable, but of course, these changes were gradual. I like this way of thinking about it:

"Human evolution is like a mosaic of change, made up of many small steps, each of which adds a piece to what it is to be human."

(Foley, 2016)

What is described as the "Great Leap" in human evolution happened around 60,000 years ago, following the near extinction of humans, who had shrunk to a small group living in Africa. Around this time, we started to develop more sophisticated tools and language; we were eating meat, and our brains and bodies had grown to roughly their current size. We started making art, sewing rudimentary clothes, and exploring broader ideas and beliefs. We discovered fire, sat around it, started to socialise, tell stories, and probably started to ponder our existence.

Can you remember the last time you sat around a fire chatting? Our ancestors' primary aim was to keep warm, ward off predators and cook food, so I imagine there would have been a fair bit of sitting around the fire. Did they experience boredom? Perhaps they poked at the fire or rubbed a stick in the sand, making patterns (as I like to do)? Maybe they let their minds wander and started to notice the world around them, perhaps perceiving it differently during the day or night or as the seasons changed. This environment would have provided a rich source for their developing, creative minds, enabling them to be curious, make connections and generate ideas. For example, "I wonder what happens if I put this leaf in hot water?" or "I wonder what I could do with this stone with a hole in it?" (Apologies for my feeble attempt at getting inside an early human mind!)

Early humans probably sat by the fire for long periods. If you were a fly on the cave wall, your modern mind might even wonder if they were a bit bored. It's not the same as sitting around the fire at scout camp or as part of a back-to-nature weekend for stressed executives. It wasn't for pleasure; it was for survival.

In this context, **waiting, noticing things and mind-wandering**, which we might label as "boredom", were essential to human development – they allowed our minds to access something different – the ingredients for creativity, innovation, and emergent ideas. For the first time in our evolution, there was something outside of merely surviving – ideas that could be explored to our advantage. Some anthropologists and scientists believe that a gene mutation or adaptation must have also occurred around this time, which changed our brain neurology slightly. That's way too complex to explore here, but sufficed to say humans started to **do** things differently.

One distinction often made between us and other animals is that we **do** things that go beyond our mere survival needs. Some might say these activities served our changing social needs, the development of culture, or because we needed to cultivate different food and use the land differently as our population grew. Of course, it is all of this and more. But what if "doing stuff" or just "doing" for its own sake is a biological necessity? (Wilcock, 1993) What if humans cannot develop and grow without sufficient doing and activity? What if our need to be occupied is intrinsic to our health and well-being?

Even in the womb, our tiny bodies start to seek activity and respond to stimuli. For example, babies can be seen responding to music heard through their mothers' bellies. Babies stretch and move against the restrictive tightness of the womb, which aids the reflexes, muscle tone, and sensory integration development. Insufficient time in the womb can result in delayed development, some of which catches up as the child grows, but some doesn't. A newborn might appear fairly inactive but is already seeking food, stimulus, comfort, and making its needs known.

Within a few months, activity (aka "doing") becomes increasingly essential to development. Heads start turning towards sounds, light, and movement, strengthening the neck and developing posture. Hands and arms begin to move, to grab, feel, and experience objects, which helps build muscle strength, grip, and fine motor skills. Activity in various environments is needed to provide these opportunities for development. Sleep is essential to rest brains and muscles. Sufficient rest and "switching off" is also required to allow all sorts of neural genesis and integration to take place and the all-important "mind wandering", which is excellent for creativity.

Children and teenagers need a varied diet of activity, just as they need a varied diet of food. As well as providing social and emotional development, activities provide sensory input essential for skill development and well-being. Our sensory system is not just the usual five senses of sight, sound, touch, taste and smell (visual, auditory, tactile, gustatory and olfactory systems). We also have spatial orientation and proprioception (body awareness), the vestibular system (body movements/balance), and a little-known one, which is very important: interoception – the sense of knowing and feeling what is going on inside your body, such as hunger, thirst, pain, itchiness, nausea, full bladder, etc. We could also make a case for other "senses", such as time perception and intuition.

Activities like jumping on the spot help activate, develop, and integrate our balance, position in space, and visual system, as they adjust to movement and our sense of touch and pressure. Bouncing on a trampoline further challenges our sensory system. It is often great for sensory integration, but only for some of us, as our systems can be quite different (Schoen et al., 2021). Cutting and sticking help develop our fine motor skills, sense of touch, ability to calibrate our movements, and hand-eye coordination. Later on, we will look at how a lack of sensory integration and regulation could occur if we don't engage and stay "bored", and how this can result in very real adult and societal problems.

Beyond activities supporting our sensory system, using time purposefully is essential to our fundamental biology; otherwise, "our brain slips into chaos and confusion" (Selye, 1976). Additionally, if we lack activities that give us a sense of belonging and connection, our health can suffer in all sorts of ways. If someone is isolated and lonely, they have been shown to have increased levels of stress and the associated health risks that follow stress (Malcolm, Frost & Cowie, 2019). They often access medical services and have more extended hospital stays (Valtorta et al., 2018). Studies on retirement have shown how the sudden loss of daily work can impact terribly on well-being (McDonald et al., 2015). Research also shows how lack of activity can impact badly on dementia, and conversely, how structured, meaningful, and engaging activities can reduce the impact (Nyman & Szymczynska, 2016). Activity is very important; it really is.

If you are in doubt about all this, think about all the elements involved in the "simple" activity of cooking a meal from scratch and the opportunities such an activity gives us:

We could cook alone, allowing us to concentrate and refine skills or maybe listen to music and let our minds wander while stirring a saucepan. We could cook with someone, allowing us to chat, socialise, share ideas, etc. We might decide we need additional ingredients, meaning we could walk to the shops, providing exercise and opportunities for meeting people on the way. Shopping also involves making decisions, problem-solving, making substitutions, and calculating what to buy (along with opportunities to develop impulse control and not come home with a massive bar of chocolate!). We might opt for a simple meal with little preparation, or we might need to chop, grate, rinse, sauté, poach, etc. – just think about all the different skills we practise for those processes and all the smells, tastes and sensory input! We also need to find, weigh, monitor, and time things, which uses our complex processing skills, including attending (attention), sequencing, searching, organising, and adjusting, to name a few. We also use complex motor skills during cooking, including bending, reaching, calibrating, stabilising, and gripping.

Cooking a meal also gives our day rhythm and structure, allowing us to experiment with food or invite friends round. It can help keep ourselves and our kids healthy, expand their palate (I failed on that one), and perhaps teach them cooking skills… I could go on and on and on.

All of this is from "just" cooking a meal.

All this body and mind activity and engagement with the process, and that's before we consider the nutritional or social benefits of sitting with others to eat.

Trust me; I'm not advocating for us all to revert to being 1950's housewives who cook food from scratch every day. I just want to illustrate why activity, why "doing", is so important and how much it can give us. Yes, we could just eat a ham sandwich every day and would likely survive. But remember – humans need to do things beyond their survival needs. We need activity and variety, not just to prevent boredom but to develop and maintain our health. Perhaps boredom serves to alert us to certain dangers in the same way that pain, hunger or fear do? Maybe boredom is saying, *"This feels unpleasant and boring – you need to start doing something else, something that wakes you up, provides stimulation to your brain, body, or soul, something that connects you to another human, something that is necessary to keep you well."*

Maslow, most famous for his model of human needs, also said the following, which to me is of equal importance:

"Capacities clamour to be used and cease their clamour only when they are well used. That is, capacities are also needs. Not only is it fun to use our capacities, but it is also necessary for growth. The unused skill or capacity or organ can become a disease centre or else atrophy and disappear."

Maslow (1959, cited in Wilcock, 1993)

In essence - do or die, use it or lose it.

Chapter 2 – Boredom: the Good, the Bad & the Ugly

"I'm bored," says the ten-year-old, three days into the six-week school holidays.

"This job is so boring," say many of us at some point.

"I'm so bored; let's go to the mall and do some shopping"

"We were bored, so we decided to book a last-minute city break."

"I'm so bored," says the teenager, surrounded by game consoles, a mobile phone and a TV.

"I'm bored, I need some air, I'm going for a drive."

"We don't want to get bored once we have retired, so we plan to travel extensively."

"Our sex life is so boring, so we are spicing it up…"

"I'm bored with my marriage…"

"Sitting in this armchair is so boring. I'm so frustrated that I can't walk anymore."

"I am so bored and sad. I have no friends, job, money and nothing to do each day."

I don't know about you, but I can relate to at least six or seven of those statements. Boredom seems to affect everyone, albeit in vastly different ways and at different stages of life (please know that I am acutely aware that I speak from a place of privilege). Boredom seems to exist for many reasons in many circumstances. Boredom seems to surface even when there are apparently many things to keep us occupied.

Before we delve into and get to grips with boredom, it's worth asking whether humans have always experienced boredom or whether it is a "modern-day" phenomenon. As soon as I wrote that question down, I thought, "How absurd, Jen – of course, boredom has always existed", but like so many things, it's an umbrella term covering all sorts of feelings and experiences and is so dependent on context. Those early humans we thought about earlier would have been busy finding food and try to stay alive, but perhaps also a little "'bored" during long, dark, winter periods by the fire? Ancient Greeks discussed experiences and feelings akin to "boredom" but didn't use that word (Bruss, 2012). Boredom has been known by other names, including "anguish, ennui, tedium, the doldrums, humdrum, the blahs, apathy, listlessness, stolidity, lethargy, (and) languor" (Brodsky 1989, cited in Raffaelli, 2018). Charles Dickens used the term "boredom" in *Bleak House*, published in 1852, which is thought to be the first time it was seen in everyday literature (McRobbie, 2021).

As civilisations developed and became more complex, boredom would have become more complex too, varying in terms of class, social status, and wealth or poverty. The ancient poets, philosophers and thinkers who wrote about what we might call boredom were likely from the wealthier classes, who had more time on their hands: I doubt they were the ones toiling all day in the fields. Roughly speaking, before the agricultural and subsequent industrial revolutions, most of us wouldn't have had the luxury of being bored. We were too busy working long hours to pay for food, shelter and warmth. Rare downtime was probably relished and unlikely felt as boring.

Advances in food production, shelter, and medicine during the 19th century meant that for some, there was an increase in freedom and choice about how to spend each day (Wilcock, 1993). We know that during Victorian times, "leisure" time emerged, and seaside holiday resorts sprung up, mostly only available to those wealthy enough to have the time and money to use them! I remember my grandparents talking about times in the early 1900s when they had their yearly "day out" to the seaside – just one day a year. Today, we have even more time, freedom, and resources available to us. It might not feel like that, but compared to an 18th century farm worker or a 19th century factory worker, we really do. However, deciding what to do with those choices, time, and freedoms seems to challenge us greatly. In modern times, some people are able craft a chosen lifestyle, something they work towards, often very different to the life in which they were raised.

Defining boredom
Defining boredom is potentially a little boring, but we probably need to, as we all experience it so very differently. Popular books focus on remedies for boredom, how to escape from it, tolerate it, or how to prevent it in the first place. Academic books are littered with historical accounts of boredom, the philosophy and psychology of boredom, definitions, classifications research and theories of boredom. It is indeed a bit dry, so briefly, here are a couple of definitions. Boredom is:

"The unfulfilled desire for satisfying activity (and) the aversive experience of wanting, but being unable, to engage in satisfying activity."

Eastwood et al. (2012)

So far, so good, but then it gets complex.

"It is perfectly possible to be bored, without being aware of the fact. And it is possible to be bored without being able to offer any reason or cause for this boredom."

Svendsen (2005, p 14)

Further complexity arises as academics and scientists try to examine, understand, explain, and categorise boredom. Eastwood and Hunter (2018) differentiate between **"state boredom"**, being bored in that moment, and **"trait boredom"**, which means having the traits that make us more likely to become bored. Doehlemann (1991, cited in Svendsen, 2005) names four types of boredom: **"situative boredom"**, such as waiting for a plane or listening to a boring lecture; **"the boredom of satiety"**, where you get too much of one thing and everything else becomes bland; **"existential boredom"**, where your soul is not content, you are bored of who you are or what life is or isn't; and finally, **"creative boredom"**, which to me sounds like an oxymoron, but it means when one is forced to do something new. Flaubert talks of **"common boredom"**, akin to situative boredom, and **"modern boredom"**, a bit like existential boredom. We also have Toohey's (2011) **transient boredom** and **chronic boredom**.

A simpler way of looking at boredom is suggested by Martin, Sadlo, and Stew (2006), who talk of **being bored at home, at work, never bored or always bored**. Here, home and work are environments with tasks that struggle to keep us active, interested, engaged, and satisfied or it's something about us – our unique make-up.

We then find studies that focus on the background factors or precursors to boredom. These might include repetitious activities, feelings of obligation, level of challenge (too little or too much), lack of social stimulation, the environment around us, alienation, depression, exhaustion, loss of mobility, loss of purpose or incentive, loneliness, tiredness, poor time management, lack of commitments, and lack of money (Martin, Sadlo & Stew, 2006). Given the breadth and depth of those definitions, it feels like there is potential for us all to be bored, with anything, at any time!

Who we are as a person interacts with our environment and the things we do, so separating those elements out has is limits, but there are some individual traits related to boredom that need more research. Martin, Sadlo and Stew (2006) suggest that this research should focus on the internal causes of boredom, such as the **inability to sustain attention, which affects engagement, flow, and the satisfaction we gain from the activity**. It is clear to me that if we stick with something long enough, we are more likely to get some benefit from it and feel satisfaction – and **satisfaction is <u>crucial</u> to not being bored**. Let me illustrate this with some examples:

- You spend the evening flicking through the TV channels, watching for a few minutes or even seconds before quickly deciding "nah, not for me/boring/same old", you might get bored. You haven't got satisfaction so far from watching TV because you haven't got into anything – you haven't stuck with the TV programme long enough, or attended long enough to see the plot, enjoy the characters, learn something new, etc. You get more and more frustrated as the evening passes by and you feel your dissatisfaction increasing. You might even hunt for some snacks, to ease the feeling of dissatisfaction...

- You start a gardening project, which requires long-term interest and ongoing attention to get results. However, plants need weeding, watering, and care, and without attention, the plants will wilt and die instead of growing and providing colour, food, scent, and the resultant sense of achievement and satisfaction. The same goes for all sorts of projects we start (hands up those of us who have lots of unfinished projects...).

- If a child has problems with attention and concentration, it can be difficult for them to sit, read, listen, or write for long periods and complete tasks. If they don't complete tasks or struggle to learn, it is difficult to get satisfaction. They also won't get the additional satisfaction of mastery or praise from the teacher or parent. Worst case, they mess around, get into trouble, and get labelled as lazy or a troublemaker.

Chronic boredom can be very damaging, can result in unhelpful behaviours, and can cause or worsen mental illness (LePera, 2011). It can induce rule breaking and risky behaviours, leading to drug abuse, alcohol abuse, suicide, aggression, crime, and vandalism, to name just a few (Iso-Ahola & Crowley, 1991; Rupp & Vodanovich, 1997; Toohey, 2011, and many more!). We'll look at that more later on.

Boredom can make us seek frequent travel, called "dromomania", and although that might not seem that bad, it's not just about flying on holiday; it's also going for a drive because you are bored or driving your kids to various "activities" so they aren't bored. In this way, our boredom, our need for variety, satisfaction and meaning, directly links to climate change. When I speak to my peers and ask, "What if you stopped flying and holidaying abroad?" they all say, "Well, I know I should, but then life would be a bit boring, wouldn't it?"

In an attempt to simplify and unite theories of boredom, Westgate and Wilson (2018) recently proposed the snappily named "meaning-and-attentional-components" (MAC) model of boredom and cognitive engagement. In this model, boredom is an affective indicator of unsuccessful attentional engagement in valued, goal-congruent activities. There are a lot of words there, so in essence, to not be bored, we need to: **attend, recruit attention, or maintain attention during meaningful activity.**

Bear that in mind for later on.

What does boredom feel like?

All of us experience boredom differently, and find different tasks and situations boring, but there seems to be some commonality of how it feels and looks. This description comes from research based on lived experiences:

"Regardless of time of life and external factors, boredom feelings were those of restlessness, combined with lethargy."

Martin, Sadlo & Stew (2006, p 194)

I immediately recognise those feelings, but decided to ask other people how boredom looks and feels to them.

Me, 49... ish

"To be honest, it's rare that I am truly bored. What I do know is when I allow myself downtime and perhaps watch TV in the middle of the day, I feel **guilty**, but at that point, I am resting or switching off, not necessarily bored. Sometimes I nod off, which is funny because as a long-term insomniac, I consider napping to be an achievement. I do find cycling on the exercise bike boring, but I wonder if that's because it gets too tough and I lack the sticking power to keep going and I get **annoyed** with myself, but I would rather be doing other things. I often get bored at conferences or talks, especially if I feel the content is 'obvious' or the speaker uninspiring, and the feelings that go with that are usually **frustration** and **irritation**, but these usually spur me to create something different, or get up and leave!"

Ava, 20

"Feeling bored and having no purpose fed my **depression** when I was a teenager. Boredom makes me feel **anxious**, like I need to be doing something, but I am not. It makes me feel like I am running out of time; **it numbs** me. It makes my head feel like it is full of cotton wool, like I **cannot think**, and I **do not exist properly**. Boredom also makes me feel **lonely** and left out, like everyone around me is having fun or has a purpose, except me. Boredom sometimes reminds me that my comfort zone isn't the best place to be. Sometimes boredom makes me over-eat, usually shitty foods, or makes me sit for hours on end, despite knowing I could find something to do – this makes me even more bored. However, sometimes boredom makes me find something to do that I usually wouldn't do, like reading a book or journalling."

Kathryn 32

"I remember hearing that phrase **'boring people get bored'** as a child, and I think I might have internalised that a bit! I like being at home. I enjoy lots of things I can do here and I've always sought to make the most of any environment, to find the fun, interest or to learn something from it. I think there is definitely something in perspective, as in, **shift your focus to find something interesting** and you will. I think spending time with children does help you harness that a bit; it forces you to notice more and find more things remarkable. The boredom I feel now is only fleeting moments, but it's usually when I'm playing the same song for the 30th time that day (I have a 3-year-old), or doing some very **repetitive** child- related activity. I used to feel boredom a lot more, when I had no children, even though I probably got to do a lot more 'chosen' activities – I did not appreciate that freedom. I mean, my partner and I reflect on this a lot; when we get some free time now to do what we want to, it's so exciting, it's like the biggest ever treat (in my case, currently obsessed with sewing clothes, his is foraging!). I also always keep in mind the thing I've heard a lot, about people benefitting from boredom to be creative, or to allow space for an amazing idea to emerge."

Richard, 54

"What is boring to me? Mowing the fucking lawn, that's boring, and I do, do that. So, yes, once a fucking week, I'm fucking well bored, fucking mowing the fucking lawn fucking every week. And I don't even agree with mowing lawns, and

I don't like having a mown lawn, and I find it very boring. So that's the most boring thing; that's the only boring thing I do.

If somebody says they are bored, I don't get it because there is so much to do, there is so much to learn. I have just got this long list of stuff and I say, 'Oh, look, why don't I study this for half an hour?' If I've got half an hour, I've got a pile of books and I just pick one that's in my mind at the moment, you know, or go for a run, but just there's just not enough hours in the day."

What about boredom in relation to some of the environmental challenges that we face?

"What, in terms of if we all had to live within one footprint, how bored would we get? I think, I think if we did it properly, we would really struggle to have enough time to do anything else. Because if you live as if there was one planet, you have to **put a lot more physical effort in**, you know. You can't keep throwing fossil fuels at stuff, so it becomes a lot more **labour-intensive**. If you've got an allotment, for example, that's a lot of work. I think, it sort of depends whether or not you find that work boring, and… and I'm not sure I do, necessarily, unless it's mowing the fucking lawn..."

Linda, 80

"I want to say I have never been someone that got bored, but I'm not sure that's true. I just **don't tolerate boring things for very long**. Looking back on my life, I moved house often and changed careers and jobs frequently. I have a CV as long as your arm and have taken more courses than anyone I know (laughs). I am a trained nurse, counsellor, coach, massage therapist (one of the first to train), reflexologist and astrologer, amongst other things. I have always been interested in different things and loved learning, but I didn't necessarily want to implement the learning or use it every day.

During my life, I have wanted to read and learn constantly. I loved conferences, study days and setting up my own groups. But it was the setting up of these things I liked. **Once the interesting bit was done, I moved on**. Running things long term, sustaining them, well, that becomes boring... so I didn't.

These days, I am so, so bored. I never really retired and was working until I was 77, but then I got seriously ill. Although I recovered quite well, I never really regained my energy and independence, and in the last year, my mobility has really gone downhill – I can no longer walk, drive my car or even get out on my own at all. I am so, so bored and **frustrated**. My hearing, eyesight and concentration have deteriorated rapidly and my daily energy seems to be spent on doing the basics like getting washed, dressed and eating etc. If I do want to do something I used to, like knitting, my hands don't seem to work like they used to. I used to read lots but now I can only concentration for two or three pages at a time. My daughter tells me to focus on and enjoy the small things, but that's so hard when you have had such a busy life."

Such a wide range of feelings, experiences, and opinions about boredom from only five people, so how could we possibly define boredom? The language used is so broad and subject to so many different perceptions that perhaps it's helpful to consider boredom as an "umbrella" term that covers a broad range of feelings and experiences:

"Think of boredom as a grab bag of a term covering emotions such as frustration, surfeit, depression, disgust, indifference, apathy and that feeling of being trapped or confined."

Toohey (2011, p 4)

Boredom, what it means to us, and what we find boring, changes throughout our lives. What I found engaging, satisfying, and motivating in my 20s is different to what I like in my late 40s. In my 20s, I liked nothing more than big parties, boozy nightclubs, busy weekends, having lots of friends, reading "chick lit" and listening to Radio 1. These days, I find myself interested in history, albeit via comedy and podcasts, and creating stuff – writing, painting, and blogging. I moved on from Radio 1 a long time ago and, dare I say it, I am now moving on from Radio 2… should I go Radio 4, Classic FM perhaps? No, I am really not ready for that.

The good bits
Apparently, we spend about six hours a week being bored (Toohey, 2011). This might feel like a bad thing, however, there are so many "good" things about boredom. Not so much chronic boredom that can be unhealthy and potentially destructive, but transient or shorter periods of boredom, which might produce positive outcomes.

The relationship between what we might call boredom and creativity is a great example. Mind wandering, the state where you are not focussing on anything in particular and not having to concentrate, is sometimes a precursor to creative insight and problem solving. Our brains need this to allow the looser, less-established neural pathways or completely new connections to take place (Runco, 2015). This state allows us to become curious, see things we didn't notice before, remember things we had forgotten, and play with our thoughts a little. It helps us notice synchronicities, incongruences, and link weird concepts. Micro-incubation of ideas take place, even though we are not necessarily aware of it. Hoffman (2017, p38) refers to these as:

"Little movements going on in the back of my mind, passing ideas which were often quite irrelevant… I called these butterflies for they fluttered in from nowhere and were gone in a moment."

Feeling bored often is not great, but we certainly need to let go a bit and soften our daily goals and activities. Unfocussed time, letting our mind wander and staring into space, can be good in moderation. This can happen when we are taking a bath, walking the dog, or stirring some porridge, but only if we don't multi-task or scroll on our mobile phones. We have to sit with and embrace a certain level of boredom, rather than immediately whipping our phones out whilst waiting for the bus or in a queue. These looser, slower, pondering, wibbling times certainly can help creativity, but also make us feel more intelligent, as we have time to think things through, reflect, and evaluate.

For artists and creatives, boredom can represent the possibility of something new arising. Sitting with boredom rather than filling the space allows us space to open up and notice these possibilities. In recent years, I have embraced periods of just sitting in my studio, staring at my half-finished paintings, flicking through old images, and letting my mind wander. Instead of getting panicky and charging on with putting paint down, I am realising that these periods of slow time result in much better work. They allow me to ponder things like "I wonder what if…?" or "What might happen if

I do this?" or "Oh, I can see something different now" or "I know what to do now!"

Boredom can also be a great teacher, alerting us to the need to change course in our lives or shining a light on our values and interests. It is clear to me that if you get bored during all your university lectures, it brings into question whether you are studying the right subject for you. Admittedly, the lecturer might not be very engaging or the work might be too easy, but if the subject is right for you, you will make allowances about the teaching or find ways to deal with it.

I also started to realise how boredom in certain tasks or situations reminds me of what I value in life, and what I don't. In coaching and therapy, we call these our "personal values", which for me include autonomy, freedom, and creativity, amongst others. A few years ago, I noticed that I was starting to get bored at certain conferences and events – things that I had previously relished. After a while, it became clear that my personal values had shifted, partly due to age but for other reasons too. My new boredom was not massive, but enough to make me nod off or become irritated and huffy during certain talks or workshops. I genuinely feel these experiences said more about me than the presenter, as others seemed to enjoy the sessions – it was me that was bored. I had moved on.

Lee and Zelman (2019, p73) discussed the usefulness of boredom in similar ways as I describe above. They found that boredom may be part of an adaptive mechanism that signals the need for a shift towards something different. That boredom may have been crucial to the development of our species, even part of the natural selection process. Today, I see boredom, frustration, and a lack of satisfaction, indicating to many people that they need to change something in their life. This ranges from small things like starting a new hobby or making new friends, to bigger things like changing jobs or retraining, moving to a new house, starting relationship counselling, or perhaps seeking a divorce.

I know that I struggle with downtime and taking a rest, but as I age, I know that pacing myself and resting is important. Our bodies need to rest, our souls need to rest, and our minds need to rest, but our over-busy lives leave us little space. Resting might feel boring, but it can provide a much-needed break from every second of our lives having to be constantly productive and meaningful.

All of this leaves us with interesting questions, such as:

- If satisfaction from a task or situation is key to preventing boredom, how can we make satisfaction more likely?
- If we feel bored, what might this boredom be trying to tell us?
- If boredom causes so many social, environmental, and personal problems, why don't health, social services and politics take it more seriously?
- Why are we so addicted to busyness, often to the point of burnout?
- Have we swopped boredom for constant busyness, overwhelm, and burnout?
- Perhaps it is possible to do less and still get enough satisfaction to not feel bored?

Busyness, a modern addiction

"Normal is getting dressed in clothes that you buy for work and driving through traffic in a car that you are still paying for—in order to get to the job you need to pay for the clothes and the car, and the house you leave vacant all day so you can afford to live in it."

Ellen Goodman

I can't remember the last time I asked someone, "How are you?" without them replying with one of the following:

"I'm so busy", or

"Yeah, I'm OK but really busy."

It was during my coach training when I started to listen to people more carefully, that I started to notice how many people reply in this way, including me. Like many human habits, we become so used to them that we stop noticing the stuff that automatically springs from our lips. The problem with getting used to saying "I'm busy" is that we start believing it. It becomes part of our natural way of being, part of our identity even, and I worry that always saying "I'm busy" reaffirms busyness as part of our identity and an expression of our value in the world.

You may be saying at this point, "Well, if boredom is a problem, surely being busy is better?" but being busy isn't really the opposite of being bored. We can actually be busy but still engaged in really tedious or boring activities. Worse still, this "busyness" and rushing around can damage ourselves and our world.

Weirdly, some people get sick when they take a holiday or have time off. This strange phenomenon is called "leisure sickness" and is more common than you would think. A study in 2002 found around 3-4% of people identified with the syndrome, whose symptoms include headache/migraine, fatigue, muscular pains, and nausea (Vingerhoets et al., 2002). Apparently, the risk factors for "leisure sickness" include an inability to adapt to the nonworking situation, a high need for achievement, and a high sense of responsibility with respect to work, alongside a large workload. In my mind, this points to an overall need to be very engaged at work and not be bored at all. I saw this first hand when holidaying on a Nile cruise with a friend who worked in the city. She didn't see much of Egypt's delights and spent most of the time asleep in her cabin, with a sore throat, which apparently was quite usual for her holidays. She didn't "do" bored, ever.

Being busy can make us feel comfortable and accepted in a world that demonizes inactivity. We can feel more justified in our daily choices to be busy when society seems to value active people, more than those who are more laid back and take life in their stride.

Outside of trying to avoid being bored and acknowledging that humans need to be occupied each day to maintain their health, why do we feel we should be so busy all the time, so much so that it risks damaging our health? Let's look at the nature of paid work and early capitalism, and what might have led to this.

"The devil makes work for idle hands."

(based on Jerome, Letter 125)

Religion and the industrial revolution both played massive parts in how we changed our view of work. The origins of the Protestant Work Ethic can be traced to the Reformation, and this led to a different take on money, work, and society. Money was seen as "hard earned" and the donation of money to charity or the poor was discouraged, frowned upon, and perceived to encourage laziness. It burdened other people and was an affront to God.

Max Weber, an early sociologist, economist, and politician, explains clearly how this social condition, combined with industrial development, marked the start of capitalism. Capitalism thrives on hard work and inequality between people. To survive, capitalism needs us to be mired in the complexity of managing daily modern life, whilst working our socks off. There was little place for idleness or boredom in this emerging capitalist world, but it did bring with it certain personal freedoms. Certain choices became apparent as wealth developed, leisure emerged and as people developed skills and trades. People could buy clothes based on fashion rather than just function. Food became more plentiful and varied, providing greater choice. People also started to realise they could change jobs, gain promotions, or even move to a different city or country. Working hard seemed to lead to a "better" life, whatever that means.

Society was changing. With more time on our hands, we could ponder questions beyond "Where is my next meal coming from?" or "Where can we shelter?" We could think about things like "Is there greater meaning to this life?" or "What is my purpose?" or "Perhaps I don't have to keep doing things this way?" We probably started to realise that life was finite and we should make the most of it. The years, months and hours of life started to gain value purely in themselves. Time became a commodity.

Jump forward to today and the moral aspect of working hard is still strong; indeed, busyness seems to be worn like a badge of honour (Gershuny, 2005). Somehow, we seem proud that our diary is full and varied, at the same time bemoaning our stress levels. I find this addiction to busyness just as worrying as our inability to cope with downtime and boredom.

I live with a man who lives in a constant state of busyness. Even if our house was completely finished, decorated and spotlessly clean, he would still find a project to do. He just looks around the house and finds stuff that could be improved or changed. He has ideas all the time. He does relax and watch TV, but not unless he feels he has earned some downtime. This means he has done a worthy day of paid work and ticked things off his job list. He hates wasting time. To my husband, playing computer games, watching films he has already seen and watching sport are all a "waste of time". Being married to him for 30 years has made me feel guilty most days for not being productive enough. I feel bad if I choose to relax and watch TV in the middle of the day. God forbid I should take a nap. I never feel I am "doing" enough, and we often have heated discussions about this. Even last weekend, we went for a long dog walk in a new place by a river, followed by a trip to the cinema and meal out on Saturday. We filled Sunday similarly and, by the evening, as I sat feeling satisfied but knackered, he says, "I don't feel like I've done much this weekend!"

The internal and external drives towards this state of busyness are interesting. I recently asked him why he constantly needs to do stuff – what he fears would happen if he stopped having projects at home or elsewhere. His responses were:

"Only boring people can't find things to do."

"I look around at the house and there is always so much to do, invent, or change."

I delved further:

"Life is short, and I don't want to waste it. I don't want to miss out on things."

"I believe that people become unfit or ill if they don't keep busy."

Of course, there is some truth in those fears. Life is finite and keeping active is generally good for our health and wellbeing, but I wonder what he will do in retirement or when he can no longer snowboard or sail or when he can't walk so well? He has already decided that retiring from work is pointless.

Don't get me wrong, for most of my twenties and thirties, I was over-busy, with a full diary at home and at work, with several projects on the go and a flourishing social life that afforded little rest. It's only in recent years I have changed – partly through necessity, partly through choice. In my early work years, I burnt out several times, had several extended periods off sick from work, and really struggled to find what we might call "work-life balance". To be honest, I hate the word "balance". When I struggled with my mental and physical health, in my thirties, my mum would say, "You need a balance. You are always rushing around being busy, taking on too much, going out too often, getting too excited, and then you get exhausted, frustrated and crash. You need to moderate your ideas, expectations, blah, blah, blah… and find a balance." I used to get so annoyed, I started to call balance "the 'b' word", but to me, balance was synonymous with another "b" word – boredom – and its friends called "accepting things as they are", "lack of imagination", "moderation", "magnolia painted walls" and "pension planning".

These days, I know that in some ways, she was right about balance. Once I untangled myself from my loathing of the word balance, I thought of it differently, more like a dynamic equilibrium, something that fluxes and flows from high to low, from busy, sparky, high, exciting, fast times, into slower, softer, quieter times, which we sometimes call "boredom".

However, we don't always tolerate those slower, quieter times very well. Take, for example, waiting for a bus. Do we breathe, take in the scenery, people watch, ponder, zone out? Or do we immediately whip out our phones and start filling up this space with scrolling and reading? I'm not suggesting we all start meditating at the bus stop, but letting our minds wander can result in all sorts of unexpected, joyful things. In that space of wibbling, zoning out, pondering, noticing, imagining, sensing, and floating lives, amongst other things, creativity. By creativity, I don't mean stuff involving paint or clay, although many artists say they need to let their mind wander at times during their creative process. Creativity means all sorts of things – coming up with new ideas, stumbling across something you had forgotten, weird light-bulb moments, improvisation, finding new connections between things, solving a long-standing problem.

If we don't accept, trust, and tolerate these wibbling, pondering, "boring", empty times, we are at risk of being less creative, innovative, and adaptable. We need to learn to value boredom and slower times, as creativity and innovation is critical to our future. As we run around trying to avoid our fear of missing out, the fear and guilt of not working hard enough, the fear of not being interesting enough, thin enough, rich enough, we risk missing out on both the big things like creativity and future innovation, but also the small things in life – those little things that give life joy, texture and meaning.

FOMO

The fear of missing out, or FOMO, as it is known by many, has a lot to answer for when it comes to our obsession with busyness and dislike of boredom. The term is not that new, but since it's been given its snappy acronym, it seems to have risen to celebrity status in today's lexicon, along with LMBL (living my best life) and other snappy acronyms. In part, the rise of FOMO must be due to social media, where hundreds of enticing images are flashed in front of us every day. On a personal level, my social media feed is full of photos of fancy drinks and meals, often cocktails or champagne or a nice cold beer, photographed on a wooden table with a sunset, Jacuzzi or some other amazing view behind it. I see images of my friends' amazing nights out, world travels, and loving couples hugging at a mountain summit. I see successes and achievements, pride in people's families, and of course, beautiful, funny pets.

However, in my more rational moments, I can see that this is actually a montage of peak moments and loveliness from about 200 "friends" all glued together, which makes me feel that everyone has all of this in their life, all of the time. It highlights what I feel I lack – what I feel I am missing out on. Of course, those social media feeds rarely show the

heartache, disasters, or tough times that make up normal lives – mind you, I do my bit by posting my rubbish hair do's, baking disasters, fuck-ups, as well as silly accidents, just to make it clear that my life is not perfect.

Of course, social media isn't the sole cause of the epidemic of FOMO. Magazines and TV shows have long since given us a view into worlds that look very little like our own.

The fear of missing out could also be likened to **envy**, one of the supposed "Seven Deadly Sins". Other people having what we want, or what we lack in some way, has often been a source of discontent, but also fuel for betterment. It can drive us to make changes in our lives and aspire to "be a better person" and "achieve our full potential", whatever the "F" that means.

Many years ago, I trained as a coach – a life coach, if you like. I chose to learn to coach as I felt it would help my work as a therapist. I didn't train for any new-age reasons such as "self-actualisation" or to help people achieve massive life goals, like becoming a film star or starting a million-pound business or other hype associated with life coaching. Life coaching sometimes gets a bad press, but I believe it does more good than we realise. Coaching is really about raising our self-awareness, learning what our strengths and values are, and also how we sometimes sabotage our plans. It is based on the philosophy that we are all creative, resourceful, and whole, rather than the medical model, which tends to highlight our deficits, difficulties, and illnesses.

One of my favourite things to ask my coaching clients is "Imagine you are able to attend your own funeral; what would you like your obituary to say about your life?" Clearly, this can be a dangerous question with ethical considerations, so I often soften it to "When you are 80 or so, what would you like to be able to say about your life?" I can hear you thinking about that right now – thought provoking, isn't it? The answers to this enquiry can make us clarify what we really want from life, what is most important to us, and can often serve to shake us into action. It can wake us up to the finite nature of life and perhaps give us a new perspective when we are stuck in situations we don't like, or indeed, if we find ourselves complaining of being bored, as we survey the countless things we could do, but don't seem to get round to doing.

Just to re-iterate, none of us have got this sorted. None of us has achieved the ideal balance between work and rest, achievement and reflection, or doing and being. Schopenhauer put this perfectly, saying:

"Life is a pendulum, swinging between us experiencing the pain of failing to fully achieve what we want or the boredom of not be able to find the will (power to do so)."

The joy of disruption and drama

I think we all know someone who seems to have deliberately created disruption or drama in their life, when, from an outward perspective, they seem to have it all – nice partner, nice home, good job, good holidays... blah, blah, blah. However, it feels as if things have settled to the point of being boring and the only way to relieve this monotony is to drop a metaphorical grenade into their lives. They suddenly announce that they are running away with the salsa instructor, giving up their well-paid law job to become an artist, moving to India to find themselves, or simply no longer wants the life they have, and that starting afresh will somehow make them feel more alive. I'm not saying it's wrong, and of course, many relationships and living situations change and shift for many reasons, but in some cases, boredom does seem to play a significant part.

I also see this happening on a small scale, such as people gossiping or stirring social situations where there seems to be no other point outside of giving them something to text, call and bitch about. It's as if they don't have other things to talk about. It's as if people getting along, accepting what is, and chatting about good things is just way too boring. Perhaps making up or inflating gossip is a way out of a boring conversation?

BORED

Chapter 3 – Boredom and Wellbeing

I found this chapter very hard to write, which is strange given that most of my professional life has involved helping people of all ages and from all walks of life, create meaningful active lives, ostensibly minimising boredom. Couple this with raising children in the age of smartphones, social media, FOMO, having a husband who is an activity junkie, an 85-year-old father who is currently ticking off all sorts of "bucket list" activities, including getting a tattoo and skydiving, and an 80-year-old mother who is bored to tears as she can no longer write, get out of the house or do most of the things she used to do. So, you would think this chapter would be easy for me to write, but it's not.

Such is the complexity of boredom, what causes it, how it persists, how we cope or don't cope, and its relationship to our mental, physical, and spiritual wellbeing, it's very difficult to unpick. Our human system is open, dynamic, and interconnected: our physical health affects our mental health and vice versa; our spiritual health and sense of self are intrinsic to our wellbeing; how we live, work, socialise and occupy ourselves all intermingle and impact in some way.

Before we start talking about boredom and wellbeing, remember that being busy and having stuff around you to do doesn't necessary mean you aren't bored. Being offered something to do doesn't automatically shift you out of boredom. Being able to engage, finding the will to act and getting satisfaction from an activity is not simple for everyone.

Being prone to boredom

Some people seem to overuse the words "I'm bored", using it as umbrella term for the ease of communication. When unpicked, they might be using it to name a variety of situations, thoughts, and feelings, e.g. I'm tired, restless, frustrated, or even hungry. Some people seem to cope with "boredom" well, whereas others don't seem to tolerate repetition, routine, or downtime terribly well at all. Some of what follows might seem obvious but if you dig deeper, it is utterly fascinating.

Toohey (2011), a prominent writer on "boredom", discusses the personal traits that might correlate with boredom "proneness". These include people who rely on getting stimulation externally from their environment, rather than generating stimulation internally. They are likely to get bored more easily and are mostly men. Make of that what you will. Susceptibility to boredom as a trait has been linked to the need for excessive excitement, with people requiring a constant and changing supply of stimulation (Gosline, 2007). This stimulation comes in many forms, as we will see later.

People prone to negative thinking may also be prone to boredom. Think of the friend who finds a problem in pretty much every suggestion you make, or one that can only see the bad side to things, meaning they stick to their usual habits and activities rather than reaching for boredom-busting variety. Toohey also cites lack of improvisation skills as a factor in proneness to boredom. By this, he means people who struggle to come up with creative responses to situations or lack flexibility and perhaps get frustrated if things don't go as they planned.

There is also a strong relationship between anger and boredom, which we will explore later. Svendsen (2005) thankfully acknowledges sensory issues in relation to boredom. He notes that sensory-seeking behaviour is often used as a coping strategy for boredom, with hyperactive people most likely to have the lowest boredom threshold. Personally, I think it's more complicated than that, as we'll see when discussing ADHD/ADD later, but **being able to maintain attention is a super-power against boredom** as it enables us to get more satisfaction from an activity.

Toohey (2011) also gives a nod and a wink to sensory-seeking behaviour, citing a German study that suggested a link between novelty seeking or risky behaviours and limited dopamine levels or receptors. In this case, the study looked at alcohol use, but other substances and activities are also seen to correlate with boredom, such as drug use and sex. I also wonder whether other activities might compensate, such as over-working or creating a jam-packed social life.

If this interests you, there is also the Boredom Proneness Scale (Farmer & Sundberg, 1986), which can help you figure out if you are prone to boredom, but there are always dangers in these types of self-rating scales. They often seem rather insensitive and unable to capture broader factors or individual traits. I also feel that being labelled as "prone" to boredom kind of feels that you can't change things and that you will always struggle with boredom. Perhaps it is possible to learn not to be bored even if you are supposedly prone to it.

I also wonder if there is some "chicken and egg" stuff going on here. What came first, the lack of activities during childhood, which limits sensory development, or exposure to a wider range of activities available in life? Or do our genes and biological traits kick in first and shape how we choose and enjoy activities?

Boredom and mental wellbeing

Thinking about the relationship between boredom, low mood, and depression seems a good place to start, as I think we can all understand this to some degree or another. Low mood, disengaging from satisfying activities, the subsequent boredom and associated loss of will to act helpfully, can lock us into a complex, vicious cycle.

At this point, it's worth distinguishing between the following: daily variations in mood, which are normal and most people navigate them successfully; melancholy – sadness, which historically was seen as normal and not pathological, unless it persisted and caused problems with daily living; low mood associated with specific life events or trauma; and clinical depression, which affects every aspect of a person's life. With clinical depression, there are many symptoms that make boredom worse, and many would argue that boredom or difficulty engaging causes depression to deepen.

During a period of depression, which of course varies from person to person, there is often a significant inability to enjoy or feel satisfaction from activities – this is known as anhedonia. If we think of our earlier definitions of boredom, gaining satisfaction from what we do is vital to not feeling bored. Depression often causes people to withdraw from the world, reducing the opportunity for activities that may help such as seeing friends, working, and exercising. Poor sleep is often part of depression – too much, too little, broken sleep or early waking. This increases fatigue, and reduces our attention span and concentration, both of which are needed in our battle to gain satisfaction from activities and reduce boredom.

Anxiety often accompanies depression, causing us to doubt ourselves, lack confidence, worry about what might happen, worry about how we come across or what people will think about us. These unhelpful thoughts are natural to a certain extent – we all get a bit nervous in certain situations or see our self-esteem struggle at times, but when they get out of control during depression and anxiety, they can cause havoc.

"I laid there on the sofa, too tired from not sleeping, too anxious about all sorts of things, too defeated by life to do anything helpful. Above all, I felt bored – bored by myself, bored with being like this and bored with my failed attempts to get going. It's the getting started that I found hardest. I just didn't have the will power to start, let alone keep going."

Anonymous

Feeling bored, having too much time on our hands, not gaining enjoyment from activities, or struggling to find the will power to do something can feed anxiety. If our mind and body are insufficiently occupied, our creative mind takes advantage of the unused mental energy and can cause trouble. Our creative mind is great at generating anxious thoughts, which pop into our mind, multiply and grow. It's one reason why letting our mind wander is good for generating creative ideas, but it's less helpful if we are not feeling mentally well, as the "gap" that boredom creates can fill with anxiety or paranoia. Carl Jung understood this well – that the birthplace of creativity is also the birthplace of "neuroses" (anxious and unhelpful thoughts and ideas). As someone who has struggled with my creativity and a long-term mood disorder, I found it so helpful when I started to understand this:

"The same process that helps us generate ten possible routes to market for a business or ten possible uses for a ping pong ball also helps us generate ten possible reasons why our daughter has not come home on time or ten tangible reasons why we believe we are being followed home by a wheelie bin."

Gash (2016)

Rarely acknowledged in depression and mental wellbeing is the need for balanced, healthy sensory input. Sensory-rich activities can be a major weapon in tackling depression and a tool against boredom, but we'll explore that later. With moderate to severe depression, it's not uncommon for people to struggle with many activities of daily life such as managing personal care, making meals, having sex, and going for a walk. Without those things, our body and its senses are deprived of all sorts of sounds, smells, tastes, sights, and other sensations. Our natural system of sensory regulation can malfunction, making matters worse – we might avoid hugs because it feels unpleasant; we might feel sick for no apparent reason or struggle with temperature regulation. This can make us avoid some sensory experiences further or conversely seek out stronger sensory input. In excess, either can be detrimental. Unfortunately, sensory deprivation can dull our senses and deepen feelings of boredom, as things seem bland, grey, and disinteresting. Our brain adjusts and our perception can become skewed, convincing us that we won't enjoy or get satisfaction from certain activities. This, in turn, makes the will to act even more difficult. It's a nasty cycle and one that is not acknowledged enough in mental health. It's worth noting that sensory deprivation has been used as a form of torture and interrogation technique for hundreds of years!

Other mood disorders such as bipolar depression and mania have an interesting relationship with boredom. During a manic phase or high mood, there can be a craving for interesting, high-octane activities, and an intolerance for boredom and boring things, people, and activities. In their fascinating work about thrill-seeking, Milkman and Sunderwirth (2009) note clearly that those predisposed to boredom have a higher rate of depression (low mood), anger, anxiety and aggressive behaviour, with some people using risky behaviours as a refuge from these more negative outcomes. Risky behaviours might include driving at speed, gambling, sky-diving or bungee-jumping, but also ad-hoc sexual encounters or drug and alcohol use. Some people who experience mania develop wild, grandiose plans for their career or a new business, and might go on spending sprees.

I know this all rather too well as we have a strong vein of bipolar illness running through our family. Some have coped well, adapted, learned what kicks things and what helps. Others struggle much more, engaging in risky behaviours that cause long-term problems or could even become life threatening. One of the problems of cycling between a low and high mood is that after a period of mania, the consequences of that high mood have to be dealt with – the debts from spending sprees, the relationship damage due to risky sexual encounters, or the failed business ideas. Dealing with these things are difficult for everyone, but if someone is also depressed, they can be catastrophic.

Another rarely acknowledged phenomenon is the relationship between boredom proneness and anger. In their research, Dahlen et al., (2004) found that those with high boredom proneness also reported aggression, trait anger, dysfunctional anger expression, and deficits in anger control, more so than those with low boredom proneness. Other research extends to find that those with boredom proneness also have a propensity to become violent or cause workplace accidents (Peters, 2016). Worryingly, we also find that boredom can be linked to antisocial or sadistic behaviour. "People grind up bugs, they dock other people's pay, they are more likely to punish people monetarily for behaving badly to others." (Preskey, 2021).

Dangerous, illegal, or anti-social activities are known as 'dark occupations' in occupational science and still hold meaning for some people. If bored, people might seek out meaning from an activity, and, as Maslow puts it, "clamour to use their capacities". These dark occupations can also be about creating identity, feeling a sense of power and control, providing money for their family, or a route back to the safety of a familiar environment such as returning to prison.

Considering gambling through the lens of providing money for your family whilst satiating other needs, perhaps puts it in a different light. In their research, Eastwood et al (2012) found a link between proneness to boredom and problem gambling, and if you think about what gambling involves, it can be thrill seeking, involves risk taking and problem solving. It is meaningful to those taking part, and its purpose and value elevated if it also provides money for your family.

Boredom eating

Kuchisabishii

> Japanese for lonely mouth, boredom eating.

These days, I recognise the times I nibble… well, more like stuff my face, because I am bored. This may not be news to you or perhaps it's just something you don't like to admit, and please know that just because I understand it, doesn't mean I don't succumb to it. Many boredom experts including Moynihan et al. (2015) and Lin & Westgate (2021) have acknowledged that people eat more when bored. This isn't necessarily eating in response to difficult emotions, but a drive to escape monotony. In a really shocking piece of research, participants were just as likely to give themselves an electric shock when bored as they were to eat M&M's (Havermans et al., 2015).

Inappropriate eating in response to poor emotional regulation combined with unhelpful self-beliefs are often labelled comfort eating. Liz Blatherwick (2021) explores this important complexity, overlooked by most diet providers and well-intentioned personal trainers. She provides great support in *A Practical Self-Help Guide to Managing Comfort Eating* (2021). If we are bored, finding ourselves in an experience without qualities, emotional discomfort arises in many forms.

"Sometimes, we experience uncomfortable or so-called negative feelings, such as anger, shame, sadness, and so on. If we are busy, we may not be so aware of these feelings, but if we stop or have a space between tasks, these feelings may begin to surface… if you are a comfort eater, your go-to feelings-blocker will be food."

Blatherwick (2021)

We can also look at boredom eating through the lens of eating for a sensory need. My husband is sensory seeking in many, many ways, including high-octane activities such as snowboarding, mountain biking and nightclubbing (yes, at

55). He also seeks strong sensations from food. Curries are rarely spicy enough, he loves whole chillies, highly flavoured foods, added spicy sauces, and eats lots of salt and sugar. Even when absorbed in a film, he will still seek out crunchy, salty, sweet, or cold snacks. You can almost see that his mouth needs something to do and is unsettled! Human beings also have a little-known sense called "interoception" which controls our internal senses, including thirst, temperature, and hunger. If our sensory system is not working well, our ability to sense hunger or when we are satiated can be altered.

So, if you are prone to boredom and have difficulty regulating your emotions or have a highly sensory-seeking system or altered sense of interoception, you may well struggle maintaining a healthy relationship to food. If you have all three, it can be really tough. Weight loss programmes and diets really need to take this on board.

Boredom and neurodiversity

Last week, I attended a lovely dinner "do", sitting around a table of eight friends, all in our 40s and 50s. I know them all well and was talking to the chap next to me, asking how his son was getting on. His son is in his early 20s and has an autism diagnosis. We chat for a bit and the conversation moves on. My eyes float around the table and I suddenly realise that at least six out of the eight people at this table meet a neuro-diversity diagnosis in some way or another. If we were to put labels on it, two have bipolar diagnoses, with one having some ADHD thrown in for good measure, and four have what used to be labelled "high-functioning autism". Some are formally diagnosed; others know they meet the diagnostic criteria but have decided there is little point in formalising it at this stage in life. Everyone works, has kids, and has the usual life challenges, like we all do. Essentially, we are a bunch of regular, irregular, middle-aged people, which is why I have a real issue with the term "neuro-diverse".

All of us, all human beings, have diverse neurology to some extent or another. This diversity affects us in many ways, including our sensory system, our cognitive system, and our emotional system. In society today, we are using the term "neuro-diverse" to describe a vast range of people, including those whose difference is only highlighted because "normal" ways of doing things, or "normal" environments, cause them to struggle. For example, school environments are regimented, requiring us to sit in rows of similar chairs, attend to verbal instructions for several hours, and teach the same curriculum to everyone, despite us all having different interests, and levels of attention etc. Most schools are not able to respond to individuality, such as highly creative children, children whose bodies need lots of movement and exercise to help them concentrate, or children who need much more peace and quiet or a slower pace.

In an attempt to help, we might assign a label of ADD or ADHD (attention deficit disorder/attention deficit hyperactivity disorder), bipolar disorder, dyslexia, or autism, to name just a few. There are many problems with these labels and treatments, that are a "one size fits all". Senior ADHD researcher at NIMH, Castellanos, noted that, "The big thing I learned was that almost none of the kids were like any others. It was almost as if there were a hundred and fifty types of ADHD." (in Gallagher, 2009, p.167)

We know that a crucial key to not being bored is being able to **maintain attention**, which helps us **engage and gain**

satisfaction from activities or experiences. If a child is struggling to attend to a task, for whatever reason, it can result in a lack of satisfaction and subsequent boredom. Remember that if something is too challenging or not challenging enough, we might disengage, resulting in worsening boredom. Add to this something called "perceptual load theory", which suggests that we will experience more distractions if the task is not very engaging (Gallagher, 2009, p167). Add to this even further that, when bored, our brain can fail to use its "executive control networks", making engagement even more unlikely (Danckert & Merrifield, 2018). In the case of a child at school, they then might fail to complete the task and/or miss out on praise or internal satisfaction. It's a vicious circle. Poor attention is a **result** of many factors, not because we are a "broken" or naughty person.

We need to seek a "just right" fit between **the person** – their neurology, interests etc., **the task** – the level of challenge, the meaning of the task, and **the environment** – low distractions, comfortable chair, etc. This is what occupational therapy, and my work for the last 25 years, has been about, and I truly wish this were mainstream knowledge and applied broadly to education, work, and other settings.

Boredom, relationships, and sex

I don't know anyone who would admit to ending a relationship because they were bored – it sounds so uncaring and shallow, implying that the other person is not interesting enough, not fun enough, not sexy enough. I feel able to say this, as this scenario has raised its head more than once in my long, turbulent marriage. Sometimes I think I was bored; more often than not, he was bored. However long a relationship has been going, the "honeymoon" period, where things were new, exciting, and interesting, eventually comes to an end. It may last for weeks, months or a few years before things start to change and feel different. The things that initially attracted us to the other person now irritate us for some reason. Each day and week have a routine and have started to feel a bit predictable. You know each other's repertoire of dinners – he can do spaghetti bolognaise, chicken curry (ready meal), fajitas for a special day, a BBQ (obviously), and sometimes a roast. You rotate between salmon, a veggie chilli for "No Meat Monday", risotto and frozen pizza (with salad, in an attempt to reduce some guilt). Introduce kids who need a degree of routine and a reasonably stable environment and it can get really boring...at the same time as being stressful. Not for all couples, not for all parents, but definitely for some. After six months, a year, five years, "it" can all feel a bit boring.

I have known many people get married partly because they seemed a bit bored, and a wedding promised at least a year of planning and weekend activities. There are trips to dress makers, wedding fairs, venues, menu tasting, compiling a gift list, finding a photographer, and so on and so on. However, after the big day has been and gone, the video has been watched five times, and the thank you letters have all been sent, a gap starts to open up. The diary is looking a bit empty, with few weekend activities planned. You have focussed on the big day for so long and you've long since stopped your hobbies. You decide you need a new project to plan... a holiday maybe, perhaps some redecoration at home? A new kitchen, a house move, a baby! Oh yes, a baby will fill those weekends and weekdays for years and years, not to mention filling those night-times too...

And what about sex?

Perhaps you have been in an intimate sexual relationship with the same person for 5, 10, 20, 30 years. Dare I say, has sex with this same person become slightly "boring"? There are so many social taboos in regard to this question. Even asking it feels wrong, but perhaps that's the point of difficult questions. Before launching into all sorts of unhelpful assumptions, long-term relationships rarely break down due to a singular reason. Let's give voice to the complex mix of possible factors, to which "boredom" adds its unhelpful weight. Struggling couples often cite things like loss of connection, low sexual satisfaction, massive life stressors, infidelity, "growing apart", "wanting different things", financial pressures, lack of spending quality time together, as some of the factors contributing to a break-up. I would also add boredom as a result of continually trying to make it work, boredom as part of low sexual satisfaction, and feeling bored with the daily routine.

Indeed, each of those factors could be seen through the lens of boredom: boredom and weariness from long-term financial problems, being bored with each other's hobbies and interests, making you feel like you are growing apart, being bored with their usual anecdotes, stories and jokes, life stressors preventing spontaneity, energy, and the ability to see a bright future together – instead, the future looks boring. Even the arguments can become boring, can't they, and I reckon we sometimes start rows because we are bored.

Boredom is definitely an understated factor in relationship problems, more often than we think. If we look at relationship troubles honestly, through the lens of "boredom", it's easy to see how our attempts to alleviate boredom can get us into trouble. We might seek novelty through another person (infidelity), a new car (a bit more debt), a holiday (a bit more debt) or new hobby, or perhaps by numbing ourselves to the boredom through substances such as alcohol or drugs. Infidelity, a longer affair, or merely flirting with someone who seems interesting, lively, or just different can easily and unfairly make the other relationship seem boring. It's so much easier to pay attention and be interested in different anecdotes, different cooked meals, different friendship groups, different sex, and different routines, than it is to re-discover interest in our existing relationship. Remember that **paying attention to something staves off boredom**.

And perhaps some boredom is inevitable in long-term relationships and maybe we could learn to love some aspects of boredom? This feels difficult though, given the age in which we live. Perhaps that might have been easier a hundred years ago, but not so much today, when we are bombarded by images on social media and TV. We seem to think that our friends have a better life, more fun, better holidays, more sex, more interesting sex, more cocktail nights with the girls, more interesting careers, etc. It's no wonder that boredom has become a much more potent force in relationships than it used to be. Maybe we should all take the Boredom Proneness Scale before embarking on long-term relationships. (oh Jen why not just suggest a whole battery of psycho-metric tests before going on a date with someone!)

Boredom, loneliness, and aging

People live longer, much longer than they used to. Life expectancy in the UK for men was roughly 40 years in 1841, for women it was 42 years, by 1920, it had risen to 56 years and 59 years respectively, and by 2019, it was about 80 years for men and 83-84 years for women. That's double the life span compared to 180 years ago (Raleigh, 2021). I find that a very sobering thought – basically, if I had been born in the 19th century, I'd probably be dead by now.

An aging society such as ours comes with many challenges as we struggle to meet needs, such as increased health and social care needs, and the need for suitable, adapted housing. Sociologists would also remind us that the changes in family structures and travel have resulted in families not necessarily living near to older relatives. Loneliness is also a big problem, as many older people live for years after their spouse has passed on or they rarely get to see family and friends (Abbas et al., 2020). Getting out and about becomes increasingly difficult, and many older people go several weeks without seeing anyone!

In relation to boredom, it's easy to see how all these factors add together, and it worries me greatly. I have seen it day in, day out during my work. I'm not going to glibly define "older age". I know many people in their fifties who seem physically, mentally, and socially older than some people in their eighties. Much as we might like to put these differences down to someone's mindset, a complex web is behind these differences, including health issues, genetics, up-bringing, housing, transport, social support. I could go on.

What we do know is that:

- Isolation and loneliness are predictors of poor health, whatever your age
- Dementia is on the increase, as is depression
- Meaningful, sensory activities can reduce the impact of dementia

- Meaningful, sensory activities can help depression

(Serafini et al., 2017; Nyman & Szymczynska, 2016; Malcolm, Frost & Cowie, 2019; Abbott, 2011; and Hidaka, 2012, just for starters)

If you are living alone and needing care support, having a different care worker popping in for a rushed twenty-minute call each morning may result in you being washed, dressed, and fed, but is unlikely to reduce boredom and feelings of isolation. It's also unlikely that you can have a decent, meaningful conversation in that time slot, especially whilst someone is furiously washing your bottom or out of ear shot in the kitchen, making your breakfast!

Being in a care home, supposedly with 24 hours' round the clock care, doesn't automatically mean you are occupied, socially engaged, and not bored. Despite calls for more activity in care homes, I have rarely seen this in action, and sadly, the people that most need engagement are often left in their rooms. Care staff who are rushed off their feet, paid a pittance and struggling to cope often say, "Well, Marjorie doesn't join in" or "It's too difficult to get Frank to the dining room for the bingo" or "Stan doesn't participate in the quiz". Probably because Stan's hearing aid has run out of battery or perhaps the quiz is asking irrelevant questions such as: "Who won the first X Factor?" (not his era, obvs) or "Who was Prime Minister at the start of World War One?" (he's not that old either). Perhaps Stan is distracted as his daughter said she would telephone, and she hasn't, or perhaps Stan just needs a poo. Helping people **engage** in activities is not easy, and if you try to get ten "Stans" into the dining room to do a quiz, it can be exhausting and frustrating for all involved.

I'm not criticising care homes, trust me. Care workers are poorly paid, despite being highly skilled, working solidly each shift, and managing huge complexities every day. I'm not criticising care home managers either. The costs and legal complexities to run a care home are massive and make it difficult to "run activities" effectively. I'm merely pointing out the sad fact that tackling boredom in the traditional model of care homes seems pretty impossible. Putting people into a sterile, magnolia-painted cube is not good for anyone, even less so for people who are unable to walk out the room or get to the pub. Covid-19 made things much worse, as activities and social events were cancelled and visitors discouraged, even banned. My heart aches when I imagine the disastrous long-term impact of isolation and boredom during this period.

We need to look at aging and elderly care differently, but it is something our society seems to close its eyes to. Perhaps it's not new or sexy enough? Scientists aren't making exciting a drug breakthrough or technological advances. Perhaps it's just too difficult or costly to solve.

Chapter 4 – Boredom and the Creation of Economy

I originally called this chapter "How Boredom Perpetuates Capitalism", but I am fairly middle class, have reaped the benefits of capitalism during my lifetime, and I also really wanted you to read this chapter. Even people who feel they are reasonably aware and alert to injustice and inequality, still equate any criticism of capitalism as sounding a bit "communist" or a bit "leftie". Besides this, the topics in this chapter go beyond boredom's relationship with capitalism. Our desire to escape boredom has more than just a passing dalliance with policy-making and social control. So, here goes my white, middle-class, privileged attempt to explain why boredom is a social, political, and economic issue, not merely a psychological one.

Capitalism, busyness and avoiding boredom

For capitalism to work, it needs us to keep busy and aspire to a "better life". Capitalism in the traditional sense is characterised by a free-market economy, with private organisations running the show, instead of being owned and run by the state; wealth and capital can be accumulated with no limits; the markets are competitive – the cheapest or best products win; the prices are controlled by the private organisations; there is a strong ideal and belief in private property ownership. For all of this to work, those involved need to aspire to something better and believe that their efforts will gain them rewards. Capitalism, therefore, is underpinned by meritocracy and strong aspirational beliefs.

The mantra of aspiration goes something like this:

"You can do anything you can put your mind to… reach for the stars… aspire for greatness."

The mantra of meritocracy might sound like this:

"Work hard and you will reap the rewards… everyone with skill and imagination can achieve the highest level… the early bird catches the worm… success comes to those of you who are clever enough, savvy enough, fast enough…"

Capitalism loves to keep us busy, at both work and home. It plays into our intense dislike for boredom by advertising the rewards of being busy, keeping earning, improving our lot, buying bigger, buying better, buying more interesting things, and nicer clothes. It keeps us so busy that we rarely have time or space to question it, let alone change it. Capitalism plays on our discontent, fuelling the feeling that other people are doing better than us because they have nicer stuff than we do, convincing us somehow that we don't work hard enough, we aren't clever enough, or the world is just unfair. It convinces us that buying a new iPhone, taking a trip to a DFS "sale" or having a new hairdo will solve it all.

The capitalist economy plays on both our desire to escape boredom but also relies on our continued burnout. We are bored and tired, so we book a weekend away, a holiday, or go for a night out. We are burnt-out, but busy ourselves even further with yoga classes, the making of kale smoothies, driving across the country for a relaxing spa weekend, finding a new job, signing up to self-improvement courses, taking up a new hobby... busy, busy, busy.

If we were all content, happy, healthy, didn't immediately grasp for a remedy, and embraced our natural boredom and slight melancholy, capitalism in its current form, might struggle. Don't forget that this is anchored into our culture by the belief that idleness is bad and the devil will find work for your "idle hands". Fear of the devil was a great way to manipulate people, helpful for growing industrialisation and capitalism, and whilst our increasingly secular society doesn't look to the devil for retribution much these days, society still shames perceived idleness. If you don't believe me, just take a look at certain newspaper headlines, which demonise so-called "benefit cheats" or "those lazy people who get it all for free".

These deep-seated social and cultural beliefs that push us to keep busy, even to the point of exhaustion, are quite addictive. Hoffman recognises that hyperactivity "can give us a sort of hedonic pleasure... a welcome sense of eventfulness and dynamism into our lives" (2007). I recognise that buzz of busyness, the satisfaction of a full and productive day with lots of ticks on the to-do list – do you?

Change for change's sake.
(and to perpetuate the economy)

I sigh long and audibly at the TV news, or when at work I hear about a new system, guidance or law being introduced, often under the advice or policy of the government. Often, the guidance is made in the name of quality, safety or saving money, but the impact and benefit are often hard to see, if not completely negligible. I also groan when I hear the phrase "new ways of working" being used, which often just circle back to what we were doing thirty years ago before it was all dismantled and is now being rebuilt under the guise of "newness". These sparkly "new" changes need new admin procedures (keeping managers and consultants busy), new admin staff (new jobs, keeping people busy), new offices and furniture (creating economy in the office furniture world), new forms for the new procedures (keeping the stationery companies in business), and new computer systems (creating new IT departments and keeping them busy, creating income for tech firms selling software and computers). We make changes for change's sake, often to alleviate boredom, creating all sorts of energy in economic systems, whilst causing damage elsewhere. Think of our increasing stress levels, the abandoned computer hardware that is no longer compatible, the masses of unused headed paper that is dumped, the meetings… the constant meetings that seem to result in zilch, nada, nothing of tangible value, except another meeting.

Breathe everyone, breathe. I am told that the above nonsense keeps the wheels of society turning.

Novelty, newness, and retail therapy
And don't forget those changes we make at home too.

Marge: *"I'm bored with how our kitchen looks – let's get a new one."* (Justified by a couple of loose drawer handles and cupboard doors that are eight years out of fashion.)

John: *"OK, it might be time."* (John might be eager for a new project, or he might be screaming inside as he contemplates the cost, effort, and disruption.)

Marge: *"I'll call in some companies to get some designs and quotes."* (Creating jobs and economy for kitchen companies and giving Marge and John weeks of fun-filled, kitchen-related shopping trips – no risk being bored, eh!)

John: *"Oh, I was thinking I could do it myself, but I suppose I can do some overtime at work over the next year(s) to pay for it."* (Instead of a project to keep him engaged at home, John gets to work longer hours at the office – lucky John! Perhaps John will be even luckier and treated to constant trips to IKEA or Kitchens R Us, over the coming months.)

Discussing a lovely new kitchen in this way may seem contentious or not relevant to boredom, but our discontent with things such as our home environment often cause us to seek out the "new" or the "novel", and in the process, keeps everyone busy, busy, busy and the wheels of capitalism turning. Perhaps making peace with our old kitchen would mean we have the time and money to do something nourishing, life enhancing, or even fun.

Here is another example, this time from my house:

Katie: *"I'm bored. I might do some online clothes shopping."* (It's August and she has been off school since June.)

Me: *"Oh, do you need new clothes? Your wardrobe seems very full."* (Such a parent thing to say.)

Katie: *"Yeah, I know, but I need a dress for the party on Friday and some new white jeans."* (She won't wear the same dress twice [FFS], and as for white jeans… we live in a house where such things don't survive long and are usually rendered unwearable after one serving of spaghetti bolognaise followed by my inadequate stain-removing attempts.)

Me: *"You already have lots of dresses – why not wear one of them? And you have at least two pairs of white jeans."* (I'm now losing the will to live.)

Katie: *"I don't like those dresses."* (AKA, I am bored of them and want the excitement of buying something different) *"and I don't have ripped white jeans"* (only intact, barely worn ones…)

She is bored with the long summer break, bored with her massive range of nice clothes, and wants to fit in with her friends at all costs. She is seeking novelty and newness from different clothes, instant reward via one-click on her phone, creating economy for online clothes companies, and let's also assume that these are not environmentally or ethically produced clothes, eh?

Busy people rebel less

Keeping busy as we try to avoid boredom and try to manage increasingly complex lives clearly benefits the economy. If you are as cynical as me, it benefits the government too – we are just too busy, too tired, and too bored to protest. As we paddle faster and faster, trying to keep our heads above water, our legs waxed, our children happy, our emails under control, our pensions managed, our diet healthy, our social life vaguely alive, not to mention our sex life, there is little time or energy left for us to question social and political issues, let alone demonstrate or rebel.

My generation are sometimes called the sandwich generation, and not because we raised the humble ham sandwich to a ham hock and mustard on sourdough bread, no. The sandwich generation are those still working full time, whilst supporting financially dependent adult children, often still living at home, and also dependent elderly parents who need care and support. Most of us won't be retiring early.

If a revolution was needed right now so we can really tackle climate change, inequality, and corruption, I doubt it would involve many of my peers. We are just too busy and knackered to even think about it all, let alone revolt.

BORED

Chapter 5 – Boredom and the Environment

Here is another rather a contentious statement.

"Constantly hearing about environmental problems and saving the planet is boring."

Yep, I see it all the time. People are starting to glaze over when the climate crisis is discussed, as if it doesn't provide us with enough excitement or novelty. Even if there is a desire to do something helpful in terms of the climate, we remain unable to galvanise the effort required to make the necessary changes. Our individual efforts feel fruitless, demotivating, and boring, and it's not great for motivation when your internal voice constantly says:

We can't change it, so why bother?

It has nothing to do with me.

I'm doing all I can.

The problems are too big to solve.

It is down to the government.

Are we bored with Covid yet? Perhaps it hasn't been around so long, not talked about for 40 years like environmental issues have been. Perhaps Covid is still a novelty, providing something to engage with on the TV, something to gossip about, something we can moan about. Perhaps, as it affects us directly, we can take individual action, feeling like it has some impact. Perhaps we need a marketing expert to re-brand climate action and make it sexy, interesting, and fun.

Perhaps we need some different vocabulary to talk about climate change, rather than use it as an umbrella term, which makes many people mentally switch off.

For some time now, I have felt that environmental groups, climate change movements and green political parties are missing something vital in their discussions. Putting aside all the essential recycling campaigns, the well-intended push for electric cars (which use huge lumps of CO_2 to produce and use gas and coal power stations to make electricity to run them), and the call for us all to eat less meat, there seems little acknowledgement of the simple truth, that our innate human need to keep occupied every day, have variety, and avoid being bored, is **central** to the damage of the environment. **Human activity and our need to "do" stuff got us into this climate change mess**, but no one seems to be acknowledging this and few are offering ideas to help people fulfil their need to "do" and keep busy without wrecking the planet.

Several years ago, I attended the conference of a political party who put environmental change at the heart of their policies. I was listening to a discussion about transport or the economy, I can't remember exactly, but they were angry and frustrated that people wouldn't just change to a more sustainable lifestyle.

"If I can cycle everywhere and not need a car, then everyone can," said the man in the beard and sandals (actually there were several of them), who clearly wasn't trying to transport a clutch of children to Brownies, in the neighbouring village, straight after school, or having to drop their kids to school before driving to work 40 miles away, working until 6pm and returning to cook a meal for everyone.

"It doesn't take much to switch to buying local produce from the farmers market and taking reusable food containers with you," said a lady who doesn't need to work full time and was able attend the farmers market every Thursday morning. Clearly someone who doesn't struggle to feed a busy, hungry family, which includes a vegan teenager, a child who only eats yellow, processed food, and a husband who doesn't eat vegetables (or pasta)!

At these conference discussions, there seemed to be a lack of appreciation about how diverse people's lives are, how complex making even one sustainable change for a family can be, and how many of our "modern-day" habits and activity choices, many of which often relieve boredom and provide meaning and purpose to our lives, would need to be dumped to radically impact on climate change. Do we dump Brownies? Do we never go abroad again? Do we accept that we can only work within a mile or two of home? Do we accept that only one parent can work, as the other has to attend farmers markets and cycle the kids to school, before returning to make homemade bread and vegetable soup?

During those discussions, no one talked about the psychology behind behaviour change, about how people's habits and daily routines are difficult to change. No one seemed to acknowledge that humans have an intrinsic need to create, do, participate, socialise, and engage in all sorts of stuff every day, often to alleviate boredom but also to provide structure, texture, and meaning to our days.

A lot has since changed in that organisation, including a stronger understanding of psychology and how it applies to the environmental challenges. There is also an emerging branch of psychology called "Ecopsychology", however, its focus seems to be more about the relationship between people, the natural world, and wellbeing, and we are still not looking at the sticky, unpleasant fact that humans need to wake up each morning, do stuff and keep occupied – this, to me, is really **the root of the problem**.

I do know a couple of families who seem to manage to live a reasonably sustainable, eco-friendly life, and as far as I can tell, seem content. I can say with certainty that they don't ferry kids around in the car to rugby or cricket or a different activity club every night. They don't go bowling, mall shopping and for drive-through food on a rainy Sunday, simply "because there is nothing else to do". They don't go on holiday abroad at all and spend a lot of time making food from scratch. One family I knew even made their own baked beans. In this particular family, only one parent was working so that the other could stay at home and facilitate this way of living, and yes, in this particular case, it was the woman that stayed at home. In this kind and loving family, there was no aspiration for a bigger house or new sofa every few years. There was no money for novelty, unnecessary new clothes or a new iPhone every 18 months.

I wish I knew what their take on boredom was, especially the kids who attended regular school and were probably exposed to very different lives to their own. I know that the kids read a lot of books (they didn't have a TV), they studied, helped out with household chores, and enjoyed the outdoors a lot. I have a feeling that boredom wasn't a concept that held much power in that household. It's not that it was deemed frivolous; I just don't think they labelled things "boring" in the same way that others might. I wondered if they hadn't even "learnt" to be bored in the first place, instead learning to accept and enjoy the slower downtimes, rather than labelling it as boredom. Then again, there were probably times when they dreamt of buying a tin of Heinz baked beans or flying off somewhere warm, but they really did seem content, and contentment seems to be a potent inoculator against boredom.

Boredom and our single-use society

I don't know about you but each week, when I put out my recycling for collection, I am stunned by how full the bags are. It varies a little, but if I have had a "busy" work week, it will be full of ready meal trays and pre-prepared food packaging (and if I have had an overly busy or stressful week, its full of empty booze bottles too). The ready meal, the sandwich meal deal, the bottled drinks, the pre-grated cheese, the ready-made houmous are all designed to save us time, effort and avoid the perceived boredom and monotony of preparing veg and having to wash up again. Many of these food products are designed with novelty and variety in mind to fend off food boredom. Imagine those "pan-seared filets of hand-reared chicken, sprinkled with unicorn dust and served with 'pommes de terre' frites" (AKA posh chicken nuggets and chips).

Ready-made food also enables us to have an uber busy life, and frees us up to do more interesting things, doesn't it? Does consuming your timesaving, microwave spaghetti bolognaise give you a renewed zest for life, or do you, like me, still settle in front of the TV and scroll through Netflix trying to find a decent film again? It can easily be argued that outside of the health benefits of cooking and the opportunities for building skills, it can also relieve boredom and provide a rich, sensory activity as we saw earlier. If only we could shift our perception of cooking, value it more, raising meal-making from purely functional food provision to become an evening's entertainment? Maybe that's my white, middle-class privilege speaking again.

Boredom is again at play with another massive environmental problem – clothing. The massive amount of water needed to make one T-shirt, plus the chemicals used to dye it, plus the transport in massive, polluting container ships, plus the transportation to the shops, all add up to a huge chemical-polluting and carbon-producing nightmare. Perhaps you were idly shopping at the mall, bored because it was raining, and you purchased a T-shirt rather than go home empty-handed, or perhaps you felt you needed to pep up your wardrobe a little, as you were bored with all your other clothes.

Boredom seems to be a frequent reason for buying new clothes, if, like my teenage daughter, you want something new for each party or social gathering. The clothes are cheap, delivered overnight, and solve wardrobe boredom in one click on the smartphone. As your finger hovers over the "buy now" button, don't forget the impact on the environment of millions of tiny one-click orders being wrapped in plastic and shipped from all over world by fuel-guzzling, polluting container ships. Amazon delivered 1.9 billion packages in 2019, increasing to 4.2 billion in 2021 – more than double the deliveries in just two years (Waters, 2021).

Please know that I eat my fair share of "single-use food" (AKA ready meals), and whilst I mostly buy second-hand or upcycled clothes, my daughters love "fast fashion". I have also tried to stop my dad buying a £3 plastic kettle when he doesn't really need a new one, but the glee on his face comes from a long-entrenched desire for getting bargains. He loves online shopping and eBay, and will often say to me, "But Jen, I haven't bought anything this week!" as I pointlessly discourage him from making yet another unnecessary, poorly manufactured purchase.

Whilst you might want to say, "Hey Jen, I recycle so that's ok", recycling is not a long-term solution. Much of what we put out for recycling each week isn't recycled for various reasons, and what is recycled uses all sorts of chemicals and carbon-producing processes.

Yes, I know it can feel a little hopeless. I can hear you sighing or perhaps saying, "What's the fucking point?" But we can't solve complex, intertwined problems with the same linear logic that created them, which is what we have been trying to do for years. We need transformational, creative approaches, which might often seem off the wall, stupid or unobtainable. Before we dismiss radical ideas, we need to remember that much of what we have invented or achieved in recent years would have seemed completely bonkers 70 years ago and probably labelled "witchcraft" 200 years ago.

Motherhood, feminism, and boredom

When I mention "cooking from scratch", I feel in danger of undoing decades of feminism, including the liberation of women from the tedium of the kitchen sink. Indeed, it feels like many of our modern-day solutions to the drudgery and boredom of housework and the relentless work of raising a family rely on things that are intrinsically bad for the environment – washing machines, tumble-dryers, ready meals, one-click delivery services, disposable sanitary towels, and disposable nappies. The list is probably a lot longer, but without those things, being able to have a career and raise a family would be almost impossible. It feels like they were essential to help early feminism to gain traction. I know that things have changed, but the domestic load is still weighted towards women. I have been on many guilt trips when, as an exhausted working mum with little time to spare, I needed to shove the wet washing in the tumble dryer instead of pinning it outside on the washing line (and then getting it in when it pissed down with rain ten minutes later). I have beaten myself up many times over the impact on the environment as I "recycle" another five or six plastic food containers… for just one meal… for just four people on this planet of seven billion people.

Is this the price to be paid for wanting an equal, diverse, and less boring life? Sometimes, it really seems like it, but outside of reasons of equality, personally, I found adjusting to motherhood, staying at home more and losing my freedom very difficult and terribly boring. My confidence suffered, my mental health suffered, and I was really rubbish at much of it. I know not everyone feels like this, but I also know that I am not alone.

The monotonous world of nappies is another great example to illustrate this complex conundrum, but we could also apply it to sanitary products or other disposable items. I recently responded to a Facebook thread about washable nappies, posted by a prominent face in the UK "green" movement. The post called for a free reusable nappy collection and washing service, to try to reduce the millions of disposable nappies put into landfill each year. In principle, I am pro washable nappies. Disposable nappies are full of plastic and the average baby gets through 4,000 of them before they are potty trained. That equates to half a tonne of carbon dioxide, with **each** nappy taking around 500 years to breakdown in landfill (Kirby, 2001). That's **per child**. It is a phenomenal amount of plastic waste and carbon, which no one is shouting very loudly about, partly I feel because using disposable nappies affords us great amounts of freedom and time to do less boring, less smelly, and more interesting things.

This debate, disposable versus washable nappies, is complicated to say the least. It's not just about choosing to use washable nappies. Washing nappies also uses water, energy (carbon), and chemicals. The production of disposable nappies is big business, estimated to have made $50 billion in 2016, and went up to $65 billion in 2021 ("Global baby diaper market value", 2022). Nappy decisions are tied up in how human beings want to spend their time each day, what is important to them, whether or not they have the facilities to wash and dry nappies, and ultimately, what they want to avoid. Soaking, washing and drying maybe 50 plus nappies a week (or 100 plus if you have more than one child under two) is pretty tedious, nay boring, and takes up time that could be spent doing something more interesting, like going to a Zumba class or having a much-needed nap! Whilst there seems less environmental impact, the soaking, washing, and drying of 50 plus nappies a week will tip even the most organised, resilient working mum over the edge. I tried with my first child but by the time she was a toddler, we were using disposables around 50% of the time. Using disposables, albeit eco-disposables, felt like a luxury and relief knowing I didn't have the time-sucking boredom of washing 50 shitty nappies each week.

As for school holidays, I mostly found them boring and stressful most of the time. My children were also bored, and I know I am not alone in my dislike for long school holidays. I used to get a foreboding feeling around the end of June as the summer holidays approached and started to structure our days, plan activities, and also help the kids find their own entertainment, as you can see from this ancient list I recently found down the back of the fridge.

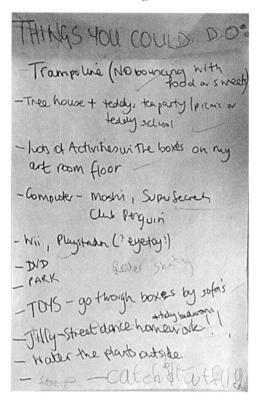

THINGS YOU COULD DO:

- Trampoline (No bouncing with food or sweets)
- Tree house + teddy, tea party / picnic or teddy school
- Lots of Activities with the boxes on my art room floor
- Computer - Moshi, Super Secret Club Penguin
- Wii, Playstation (? eyetoy?)
- DVD   Roller skating
- PARK
- TOYS - go through boxes by sofas
- Jilly - Street dance homework!! tidy bedroom
- Water the plants outside
- soap — Catch it up!!!

Boredom and travel

Alongside sex and drugs, travel is apparently one of the main ways we humans try to alleviate boredom. Travel, whether it's flying abroad for holidays, driving to LEGOLAND® for a boredom-busting family day out, or going for a drive to escape the house, it's all problematic for the environment.

Using travel to alleviate boredom is not a new thing either. With the advent of accessible rail travel and steam ships in the mid-1800s, travel became easier if you had the financial means. If you were a wealthy, young man during the late 17th to 19th century, you might expect to go on a "Grand Tour" of Europe or further afield. If you were wealthy, didn't need to work, and were bored during the 19th century, you could choose to travel frequently and might even be labelled a "dromomaniac".

Dromomania means having an addiction to travel, but I would suggest it is no longer just a wealthy, 19th century thing. I have numerous 21st century dromomaniacs amongst my friends and none of them are particularly wealthy. During my twenties, I was probably one too. Low-cost air travel has made frequent travel available to many people. Even in my lifetime, it has massively changed from the 1970s, where only the posh kid went to Spain once a year for a holiday, to several of my daughters' friends taking multiple foreign holidays each year as a family.

We yearn for difference, a break from routine, a break from the boredom of months and years of work stretching out in front of us. We often plan our holidays in advance to punctuate our year with variety to make our boring or stressful jobs more bearable. We often go out in the car and like to explore new places, again feeding our need for variety and to avoid a boring day indoors. I don't feel brave enough to ask whether you sometimes get bored on holiday or on family days out. I know I sometimes do, but let's keep that one to ourselves, eh?

Frequent travel is not a great strategy for coping with boredom, is it? Not when we are supposedly meant to be

tackling climate change. One flight to New York from the UK requires someone to recycle for five years just to off-set the carbon. Car use has grown exponentially since the 1950s. I remember my dad telling me that when he brought his first car around 1955, his was the only care in the road and he lived in London! Before you start yelling at me about electric vehicles, it still takes lots of carbon to make new cars and apparently, our power stations can't produce enough electricity for us all to have electric cars anyway!

A different focus

For many years now, I have seen that tackling a problem head on sometimes causes it to grow or make it worse. I'm not saying that at a government level we shouldn't be taking "big" action or political action to tackle things, but in terms of our day to day lives, I have found something different to be helpful. In my extensive coaching and therapy work, sometimes the "issue" brought to be solved doesn't end up being the real problem.

Let me explain more.

I have lost count of the times when someone has come to me saying, "I want to end my marriage", and through exploring, imagining, evaluating themselves and their lives, they usually end up saying, "Actually, the relationship isn't the problem... I need to find a new job/reinvent myself/move house/find a new purpose."

The problem wasn't the "real" problem, and the answer wasn't the linear, obvious one of "get a divorce".

I feel the same about climate change. Hitting it head on isn't working, and in some ways, our CO2 output, pollution production etc. have actually worsened. We need to explore the problem from different angles and tackle it at a human level. We need to design a "new future", not take action based on a "used future".

Sohail Inayatullah is a futurist and UNESCO Chair in Futures Studies. He studies the future, how we perceive it, what we aim for, what we assume about it, and how that all shapes our current actions and plans. He talks about how our governing bodies make policies and plans based on a "used" or second-hand future. A "used future" being one that is worn out, of no use, or irrelevant to our time. He describes these second-hand futures as inherited from a previous generation and a previous set of values, desires, and needs, often with outdated knowledge and assumptions. Future town planning is given as an example: if we place the need for speedier travel as a main objective of "good town planning", assuming that it will help business thrive and make us all happy, we will prioritise building bigger roads, carve up green space to create car parks etc. Another aspect of this particular "used future" involves doggedly sticking to the dominance of the car, thinking the solution is to change to electric cars, but as we saw earlier, this just pushes the problem elsewhere.

We need to design and work towards a "new" future. We could craft future plans that recognise that people need to wake up every day with stuff to do - that people need to engage in meaningful activity, keep occupied not merely distracted, be active, connect with people, animals, and nature.

It will require bravery, creativity and some serious internal change.

BORED

Chapter 6 – A Way Forward

"All of humanity's problems stem from man's inability to sit quietly in a room alone."

Blaise Pascal, Philosopher

I hear you, Pascal, but I prefer my version:

"All humanity's problems stem from our inability to understand ourselves, including our innate need to be occupied, engage in meaningful activity, and respond positively to what we might call boredom."

Jen Gash, boredom tamer

Why we need to take boredom more seriously.

Trying to make a case for the importance of boredom might feel superficial, perhaps even sound like a "first world problem". At first, it might seem glib, or even indulgent, but I am hoping by now that you have started to see how our relationship with boredom and our basic human need to be occupied is at the root of **many** problems, from physical and mental ill health, obesity, climate change, unchecked capitalist activities, economic inequality, and even aspects of modern slavery. It's not a straightforward relationship either

– it's systemic, complex, intertwined, and change might feel completely impossible.

This complexity is important to understand as it can stop us from even attempting to make a change. You hear yourself saying "this is too difficult" or "I am already in overwhelm and can't cope with anything else". Perhaps we start to realise that the change we are trying to make might have unintended consequences. As we have already seen, solving or avoiding feelings of boredom through making ourselves busier, driving to a corporate gym, booking a few city breaks, or starting your own business (AKA "busy"ness), can help at one level but at the same time feed capitalism and accelerate climate change. Sorry… not sorry… some things have to be said. Yes, we get bored. Yes, we crave novelty and a change in the routine. Yes, we have an innate need to keep our hands, hearts and minds occupied. Yes, we have a natural desire for variety, social connection, fun, and exploration, AND surely, our natural creativity and adaptive skills could be channelled into more positive ways forward to manage these complex, perhaps unfulfilled needs we call boredom?

As I write, we have loosened pretty much all of the restrictions of the Covid-19 pandemic. During the first lockdown, hope was expressed that we might see Covid as an opportunity for change and not go back to excessive car use and flying. Perhaps we might continue to look out for and shop for the elderly and isolated in our community, or we might remember those "boredom" relieving activities we developed at home, which meant we weren't always rushing "out and about". However, change doesn't happen overnight; it doesn't happen in 3 months or 18 months. Whilst the political parties and media continue to argue about learning the lessons from Covid-19 and blaming each other for mismanagement of the pandemic response, I think there are broader things to reflect on.

How we responded to these Covid19 lockdowns, restrictions, limitations, and social "rules" was fascinating. We all had to adjust, some more than others, but everyone had to find new ways to structure their daily lives. We were resourceful and adaptable, and much of this was due to having to change our perceptions and feelings about staying at home, our daily diet of activity and about boredom. Yes, after several months, even I needed to get out and was desperate for a pint whilst propped up against a sticky pub and what a pint that was when it finally arrived. However, I am aware that I didn't really feel **that** bored throughout the whole pandemic - I found plenty of things to do to occupy myself.

And I wasn't alone. During the lockdowns, I saw people decluttering their homes, decorating, gardening, building things, finishing long-awaited house renovations, starting new craft projects, and finishing old ones. They had online quizzes and parties with their friends. Jigsaws, board games and sewing machines resurfaced; mind you, I reckon a fair few people had to Google "How to thread a sewing machine"! I don't know about you, but mealtimes took on greater meaning and I even got excited when the post was delivered.

Little things seemed to matter more.

I saw people walking much more, both as families, and on their own. I saw family dogs that were getting so many walks, they must have been knackered! Home offices were quickly crafted out of kitchen tables, dressing tables or any free surface. I saw people calling on elderly or isolated neighbours who had to quarantine, taking them meals, doing their shopping, and standing on the doorstep for a chat. Not being able to travel, we explored our local areas, finding places we never knew existed. Not being able to go away on holiday, we embraced staycations and the summoned the creativity needed to fill several days and find activities close to home.

I know that this is rather a rose-coloured, privileged view of it. I know that subscriptions to Netflix and Amazon Prime rocketed, that there was an increase in domestic violence, and of course that many people died. I am acutely aware that I live in middle-class, middle England, where people have gardens, generally nice neighbours and reasonable WIFI, but if you are focussing on that, you are missing the point. I'm not downplaying the loss, fear and anxieties, the isolation and loneliness that many experienced or the possible long-term effects on mental health. I'm just casting a different gaze over what happened during the times of restriction, which meant that we had to stay indoors, change our daily "doings" and adapt rapidly.

Adaptation – a human superpower

We all had to adapt during the lockdowns – there was little choice. There was huge potential for boredom, but many people I spoke with said they rather enjoyed the different pace and shape of their daily lives! Being able to adapt involves recognising the changes afoot, having the creativity to explore and generate new ideas, having flexibility and resilience in good measure, retaining a sense of humour, all served with a dollop of acceptance about whether or not we could change the situation. This is not passive acceptance or pessimism where we say, "There is nothing I can do… I am powerless… this is all happening to me", but a wise acceptance of what we could do, a willingness to let go of what we couldn't change and tenacity to place our energies where they would have the greatest impact.

Sometimes we are forced to adapt, sometimes we choose to adapt willingly, but our natural ability to adapt is a human superpower and a great weapon against boredom.

Although I risk making this sound like a self-help book, which was never my intention, it wouldn't be great to identify a big problem like "boredom" and not offer some ways forward. There are selfish reasons for this too. Among my close friends and family, many seem to have problems that relate to boredom, from moving house frequently, not sticking to jobs, problems with obesity and mental health issues – the list is long. So, in the spirit of exploration and helpfulness, hopefully the following doesn't sound preachy. Please know that my life is as complex, messy, and imperfect as the next person, but I rarely find myself bored these days. One of the most helpful things I have done was to explore my perception of boredom and my personal relationship to it.

Aware and mindful

Whether you want to be "less" bored, tolerate downtimes better, reduce your compulsion to be constantly busy, stop boredom eating, or finally get round to doing the things you really want to, it all starts with you – how you notice, perceive, process, and talk about boredom. We need to find out what we find boring, why, and what we keep doing about it. It's helpful to notice whether we get bored with things that others don't seem to, and vice versa. We need to become aware of our own traits such as inattention and impulsivity, which can impact on boredom unhelpfully. We need to do a bit of a life audit and see where, in the past, boredom has led us to do unhelpful things such as spending too much money, buying things we never use or starting hobbies we abandon quickly. Perhaps we have too many choices, too many options, too many clothes, too many hobbies, too much of all sorts of things – this can lead to boredom as we find less meaning in things. We need to be very, very honest with ourselves.

Understanding our own, unique sensory profile may also help us understand what our body and mind need in relation to boredom and explains why we crave certain activities. For example, if you are someone who could be described as "sensory seeking", you might like spicy foods, fast-paced activities, firm pressure on your body, loud music, and vigorous dancing. Without enough of these strong, stimulating sensory activities, you can feel out-of-sorts, restless, discontent and bored. Completing the Adult Sensory Profile (Brown et al., 2001) might help identify what your sensory needs are and how that might explain the activities you crave. It may be that you are actually sensitive or avoidant of sensory input or have a very low registration of sensation. All give us good clues about ourselves, the activities we seek and the ones we try to avoid.

As we have started to acknowledge, the word "boredom" is an overused blanket term and covers a vast array of feelings, sensations, and thoughts. The problem with using a blanket term is that it gets over-used, distorting our overall perception. If we say we are bored to every feeling that could be vaguely labelled as boredom, we might find ourselves saying we are bored 10, 15 or 20 times a day. Even if we are just saying it to ourselves internally, our brain still hears a mantra of "I'm bored" and becomes an **expert in feeling bored**. Shortly we will see how this happens, and how our brain is shaped by what we practice - our daily words, thoughts, and actions.

Figuring out what we are really feeling, instead of lazily and repeatedly labelling it as boring, can help us stop over-identifying with boredom. Next time find yourself saying, "I am bored" or "This is boring", run some of these questions through your mind:

Am I bored, or a bit tired and need some downtime?

Am I bored, or is this task/activity too difficult to get satisfaction from?

Am I bored, or is this too easy for me to get much satisfaction from?

Am I bored, or perhaps my body needs to move, run, stretch?

Am I bored, or am I lonely?

Am I bored, or am I unable to attend/concentrate enough to gain satisfaction from what I am doing?

Am I bored, or do I resent the thing I am having to do?

Am I bored, or am I yearning to distract my mind for some other reason?

Am I bored, or is my sensory system under-stimulated?

Am I bored or is my sensory system overstimulated, making concentration difficult?

You might find it's a combination of these.

As well as acknowledging that we are very much human "doings", having our "being" occupied is also important. Having our **"mind full"** doesn't necessarily mean our brain has to be busy with thinking or tasks. **Mindful**ness, a popular meditation and relaxation technique, has an important role in boredom. During mindful activity, you bring your whole attention to your senses, noticing what you can see, hear, taste, smell, and feel at any one moment. You are invited to stay in each moment and ignore your mind's distractions as they pop in. Kabat-Zinn (2017) calls this "open hearted, non-reactive attending". This increased awareness when at rest and also during activity fills our mind, reducing the impact of distraction. Lee and Selman (2019, p71) noted the importance of this:

"Acting with awareness may mitigate boredom's effects by strengthening attentional systems or by reducing boredom's aversiveness."

Giving our full attention to a task, conversation, or activity serves other functions too. If we keep avoiding quiet times or downtime it may be because we dislike our brains having too much time to think. If unchecked, this can turn to anxious and paranoid thoughts, or we might respond by keeping constantly busy and rushing about in the car. It also does little to strengthen our boredom muscles. Instead, we could provide our brains with something healthy to chew on, something to do that takes focussed attention and leaves less space for worrying or boredom.

Noticing and responding differently

Regardless of what answers you might give to the above questions, we all respond to uncomfortable feelings, even if our response is to do nothing. In those moments of discomfort, unpleasant thoughts, or fears, we basically have three ways of responding: fighting, fleeing, or freezing. If this sounds familiar, it's an extension of the well-known "fight or flight" mechanism produced by one of the oldest parts of our brain, the amygdala. The amygdala serves to protect us from real dangers such as an attacking tiger. Interestingly, our brain can't distinguish between real and imagined fear. The addition of "freezing" acknowledges that we sometimes respond by doing nothing. This might be a conscious choice, or immobilising fear, overwhelm, or even indecision! Today, we rarely find ourselves facing a hungry tiger, but our mind still responds to fear and unpleasant emotions in similar ways: do I run away, withdraw emotionally, or avoid the emotion (fleeing), OR, do I do nothing out of fear or overwhelm or intentionally ride the feeling, wait and see what happens (freezing), OR, do I take action, immerse myself in what's going on and engage fully (fight). These relate directly to how we respond to boredom.

Fleeing: we sense boredom and run away to do something else, be it buying something, eating/drinking something. We might book a holiday in anticipation of future boredom or book a last-minute weekend away to flee immediately!

Freezing: we might not realise what is happening and start getting angry, upset, or low. Alternatively, we might intentionally zone out, ride the feeling or watch it with curiosity. We might learn to enjoy the feeling, deliberately allowing it, noticing the positive things that could emerge.

Fight: we could be proactive, immerse ourselves further in what is going on around us, deepen our sensory experience, find interest in ordinary things, and resist labelling it as boredom. Instead of trying to avoid it, we could get engrossed.

Once we start to recognise what is really going on inside our "bored" mind and body, we can acknowledge how we usually respond, and whether we want to react differently.

"I thought I was bored, but realised it's not that simple. What could I do instead of snacking or having a gin that might make me feel more content?"

"Actually, I am not bored, but I am a bit tired. Perhaps I just need a rest for half an hour."

"It's not that this coursework is boring, it's just not challenging me enough to keep my attention. What could I do differently?"

"I said I was bored, but I think my body is restless and I need to go for a walk before I try and get into something."

Do I make it sound easy? I know that's not always the case. I'm often in that same place, sitting on the sofa, feeling a bit lacklustre, a bit stodgy, some might say demotivated, but the words "I'm bored" spring from my mouth instead. I am struggling, but I do have choices – I could find the will or motivation to do things differently, I could relax and enjoy the downtime, or I could continue moaning about feeling bored (by the way, moaning to yourself still counts as moaning!).

As we saw earlier, the problem with continued feelings of boredom and the associated internal monologue is that this becomes a thinking habit that shapes our brain and we become experts at being bored.

Attend, engage, and sculpt your brain

Years ago, we used to think that our brains couldn't change, but advances in neuroscience have shown that our brains can adapt, form new connections and be shaped. This is called "neuroplasticity" and ultimately means we can change our perception, including what we find boring and how we experience enrichment, fulfilment, and contentment.

"Neurogenesis", the growth and development of neural tissue, is part of this process and is a circular process – variety and enrichment help neurogenesis, meaning we can hopefully experience more satisfaction.

To build new neural pathways and "rewire our brain", we need to practice and repeat the thoughts or actions **we want**, rather than practising what we don't want. Think of our ability to manage boredom as a muscle – if we don't exercise it, it gets flabby and weak. Practising being interested, engaged, and giving full attention to things builds our anti-boredom muscles; however, if we feed ourselves instant gratification and fast fixes, our ability to manage boredom becomes weak. Savouring does the opposite. It means enjoying the activity, making it last, squeezing out all the good stuff, breathing in the satisfaction and not rushing onto the next thing.

Interestingly, our brains struggle to differentiate between real and imagined experiences, but we can turn this to our advantage. You can savour past experiences, such as recalling in detail a swim in the sea – an immersion memory that helps shape your brain and simulate the real thing. Savouring and keeping a gratitude journal are two of the strategies used by positive psychologists to build happiness and resilience (Miller, 2019).

We also need to strengthen our ability to switch between our brain's default network, which is a set of regions more active during passive tasks like mind-wandering, internal rumination, and automatic responses – we could call this mind-empty, and tasks demanding focussed, external attention – which we could call mind-full.

Different and doable

"We cannot solve our problems with the same thinking we used when we created them."

Einstein

There are many ways of interpreting this Einstein quote, but for me, it's simple. In relation to boredom, if we try to solve it head on, by doing more, being over busy and continually finding ways to distract ourselves or avoid discomfort, we might succeed in the short term, but at the expense of the longer term. Our feelings of boredom exist as one small part of a complex, intertwined system – our modern lifestyle, an infinite choice of activities and opportunities, a yearning for more, combined with a creative, rather anxious, and definitely complex mind. If we are not careful, we might make it all worse. We might develop an increased need for distraction and novelty, increasing our feelings of boredom, with the resultant damaging outcomes such as increased car use, consumerism, climate problems, or relationship problems.

Outside of the internal shifts discussed in the last chapter, here are some small, practical ideas that have the potential for multiple wins. By multiple wins, I mean they have the possibility of reducing our feelings of boredom AND improving our wellbeing, relationships, cause less damage to the environment, and other good things. Where it felt important, I have also acknowledged and included ways of reducing possible barriers to these ideas, and hinted at what we might need to reconsider as a society.

Less boring ways to keep well.

What happens when you think to yourself "I really must get fit, lose weight and improve my health and wellbeing"?

My immediate thoughts are "ugh… driving to and from the gym – boring and it uses up my petrol…" or "ugh, boring, bland, ready-made diet meals" or "ugh, a boring evening at a slimming class", and importantly, "ugh, I am too busy and can't fit in five trips to the gym and make myself different food for the rest of my family!" We then make our wellbeing pursuit even more complicated by adding in another activity. Perhaps something for our emotional wellbeing. Perhaps a smattering of therapy or life coaching. It can all get a bit stressful, not great for wellbeing…just saying.

However, we could make activity choices that are **simpler, less boring** and result in **multiple wins.** In 2008, the New Economics Foundation developed the Five Ways to Wellbeing (Marks et al., 2008) to help people take action to improve their wellbeing. These Five Ways are: **connect with others, get active, learn new skills, give to others, take notice** (be present to the moment). What follows are some ideas that provide **wellbeing on multiple levels**, without going to the gym or donning Lycra, and are often free. Recruit your natural creativity by taking each idea, making it yours, and finding all sorts of different ways to spice it up. If you find your inner unhelpful voice saying, "that's boring", challenge this thought, this perception, and notice something different every time you carry out the activity.

Walking: on your own, with a friend or family. You could walk with a podcast on your phone, or music. You could walk with your dog or walk someone else's dog, someone who can no longer do it themselves. This also scores you wellbeing points on the "give to others" front. If you find yourself looking outside at the weather and thinking "nah... too cold/too windy/too wet", challenge this thought. Remind yourself that weather can make a walk more interesting – leaves blowing, clouds racing, reflections forming on puddles, frosty shapes on plants – I could keep going. It also gives our sensory system a boost as our temperature regulation system needs to work, we feel sun/wind/cold/rain on our face, and we can smell different things. I could keep going, but reckon you see what I mean. Walking is very underrated.

"We found that happiness is highest in places with many activities going on (cafés, restaurants, shops, traffic) and many people being around. Hence, stimulation turns out to be a specific need that can be fulfilled by walking in urban areas. However, in support of restoration theory, we find that places with lower activation levels may also foster positive feelings, especially if they contain natural elements (such as trees and water) or buildings with a more contemplative character."

Ettema and Smajic (2015, p7)

Dancing: a good ol' boogie at home in front of the TV is free, and you get to choose the music, or dance in a group, and you will get fit, see your friends, and could even dress up. Even better in a group at the pub! Start small, just doing 5 or 10 minutes, and build up from there. Then, of course, there is ballroom dancing, line dancing, square dancing, or ballet (yes, there is ballet for adults), burlesque, or pole dancing. Dare I suggest Morris dancing, which is great for fitness, fun, and stress management especially if you do the stick banging one, which often includes pub visits. If you don't have a Morris dancing group locally, you could start one! You might hear yourself saying, "I'm not doing that, I feel daft" or "My family will make fun of me", and if those are the main worries, dance with your headphones on, out of sight, or just say to yourself, "I really don't give a fuck." If you find yourself saying, "I don't have the space", I reckon we could all boogie in a very small space at home, even if it is the bathroom. If you find yourself not getting round to doing it, make it easier and smaller – perhaps stand up and dance for three minutes during the TV adverts. Don't see it as an additional thing to do; combine it with a girls' night in, or a film night or other social evening. Monday evenings are good for exercise… nothing much happens on a Monday.

"We found that dance with interactive, live music provides feedback that also increases levels of endorphins more than dance without live music."

Jola and Cameiro (2017, p28)

Skating: roller-skating in your neighbourhood instead of walking. No need to drive or spend money after you have purchased your own skates. Maybe attend roller skating at a leisure centre or hall. That way, you also get music and meet others.

Swimming: swimming in the local pool is most people's go-to, but so many people I know are starting to swim wild. Wild, cold water swimming ticks many boxes. Its low cost and sociable, and many physical health benefits are being reported.

"As a swimmer, there was a natural continuum from the urge/instinct (affectively embodied. mood dependent) to go for a swim, the smell of the swell and the building excitement/apprehension as the water came in to view (affectively/emotionally sensed and accessing a stirred body memory), the shared experience of undressing and entering the water (mixed emotions of remembered coldness and preparing the body for the water) and the strange noises emitted during and after the swim (as expressed emotion and body-shock)." Foley (2017, p 7)

Cycling: regular, outside cycling is best for reasons beyond wellbeing as we will explore later, but being outside can also help regulate your sensory system, which is vital to wellbeing and to managing boredom. Road cycling also challenges our balance and vestibular system. I'm not against exercise bikes at home or spin classes, but attending classes require us to drive, again, and the thousands of second-hand exercise bikes for sale should really tell us something.

"Findings indicate that green-cycling served to enhance the participants' sense of wellbeing and in doing so, helped them cope with the mental challenges associated with their lives."

Glackin & Beale (2018, p 2)

Get moving: Have you heard about Green Gyms? Many parks now have items of gym equipment that are outside and free to use! What about gardening? Mowing the lawn is good for building arm muscles, and whilst a one-off digging binge can be hell for our backs, if we do it in small doses and regularly, it can really build wellbeing (unless you are Richard on page 31). Jepson (2016, p.157) found that Carol, a participant in "The Garden Project" who had suffered from depression, said that it gave her space to breathe, and a gratifying activity to complete.

What about home yoga? There are hundreds of free yoga videos on YouTube and a yoga mat is pretty cheap. Yoga hits many wellbeing points, including breathing, mindfulness, sensory integration, stretching, muscle building and stress relief (Harvard Health, 2020). What about archery? It's good for upper body strength, posture and useful in the event of an apocalypse.

Outside of physically challenging activities, don't forget other things we have to do every day can also contribute to our wellbeing. Remember our discussion earlier in the book about cooking and how it gives us so much more than just food? Other daily activities can help us build wellbeing. I want to add housework such as hoovering; however, I think that might make some of you cry or shout at me...

Rethinking Reading

Sitting down and reading a "real" book may sound slow and boring to some of us in today's fast, multi-media, multi-channel world with its immersive experiences, binge watching and binge listening. However, perhaps there are ways we could fall back in love with reading as this young adult has:

"I used to think reading was boring, but now I am completely in love with it. Around 2 years ago, I realised that I didn't have to read the books that everyone kept saying were good as I found them boring. Instead, I explored different, non-traditional genres such as ergodic fiction (look it up). First I thought about what types of films and TV shows I loved watching then used Goodreads (www.goodreads.com) to explore similar book genres. I read the book reviews rather than the numbered ratings as I found that often my favourite books were rated low. This helped me get a feel for what the book would be like and what to choose. I went from taking months to sluggishly read romance books, to speeding through sci-fi/psychological horror/thriller books in less than a week. I could really immerse myself and found that reading also helped my sleeping habits. I used to lay in bed for at least an hour every night before falling asleep, but now I read in bed and often fall asleep within 20 minutes. On the environmental front, 90% of the time I get my books from

World of Books (www.wob.com) which are all second-hand and much cheaper than new books, which is important as well, as I have significant university debt!" Lizzy 22

Did you know that reading can also improve empathy, reduce stress, grow your vocabulary, improve mood, and strengthen your brain's neural pathways (Hansen, 2020).

I reckon you are getting the gist of this – how we can make seemingly ordinary activities more active, interesting, varied, and easier to do. We have to get ourselves out of the various thinking ruts that can trap us, including challenging our perception that things are boring or that there is only one way of doing things.

Less boring ways to learn.
If we see boredom as a state of under stimulation or having insufficient challenge, or the opposite where something is too difficult for us so we "switch off", learning in a traditional school environment presents many problems. If I had my way, schools would have the freedom to design their own curriculum and tailor it to different children's needs. In general, classes would be smaller, the whole school would be smaller, and this would make adapting teaching to individual needs easier. Smaller, quieter schools would also help the children who struggle with noisy, over-stimulating environments, which many more kids struggle with than we realise. Learning would be practical and sensory-based up to around 7 or 8 years, focussing on cooking, music, gardening, art, movement, and learning about ourselves as human beings and the world we live in! The kids with dyslexia, inattention or other "learning" issues would not be left behind so easily. This approach wouldn't dramatically change overnight when the kids were 7 or 8 years old. Traditional

literacy and numeracy would be introduced but in the context of projects, exploration, and daily living skills. Some educational settings already embrace these more varied, more practical, more sensory approaches to learning, including forest schools, Steiner schools, the Montessori approach, and home-schooling.

Trust me, this would be way less boring, and build happier, healthier kids.

I can already hear you saying, "But what about their GCSEs, Jen? Those kids would be way behind." Well, yes, that would be a problem if you only change one end of the system for younger children and expect them to merge with the old system of "treat everyone the same from 16 onwards".

If the function of education is to streamline the manufacture of young humans so that they all have similar characteristics and levels of "learning" when they are ready for the workforce, then fine, we should carry on as is. But I really don't think it is working as well as we would like to believe. Mental health problems in young people are rising dramatically, self-harm continues to rise, and lots of kids are refusing school or struggling to cope in "normal" school settings. Schools really to stop being production lines (check out Ken Robinson for more on this).

As we saw earlier, being able to pay attention to something is a superpower against boredom, so helping children and other learners show up, participate, attend, and engage needs to a priority. People often need help when they start doing something new. Think back to when you started a new hobby or activity, perhaps a new group or class. If it involves a new skill, it's likely you will be rubbish at first. You will need to learn the rules, build skill or perhaps build stamina. It can be uncomfortable, but someone encouraging you to come back and keep trying can make a huge difference to continued engagement. We have to keep showing up to get increased levels of satisfaction. If we bail after one try, we quickly learn that it was dissatisfying, not for us, or boring, which may be completely wrong. Had we kept showing up, been encouraged, given more support or different ways to learn, our ability to attend and gain satisfaction may have built. School should facilitate this by engagement in activities that stimulate us to take notice, spark interest and bring out our natural leanings. Primary and pre-school settings are good at this, but it seems to get lost at secondary school.

I reckon many of you know this to be true.

Who doesn't know someone who "didn't concentrate" or "refused to engage" at school but as an adult flourished when they found flow in a different discipline, or at 40 years old found out they had undiagnosed dyslexia, ADHD, or something else?

Less boring ways to work
I remember studying Sociology at school and reading theories postulating that in the future, there will be less paid work available and more leisure time. As that was back in the 1980s, it would seem that we are now in the future (!) and the impact of technology has been farther reaching than those sociologists could have imagined. The accessible global market has seen production of many goods shift to different parts of the world. To give one example, in the UK, we now manufacture very few motor cars. Customer service industries such as call centres and technical support services don't need to be in a specific place. Online portals, online

booking, ordering, and various "lean" initiatives have reduced the need for many traditional jobs. You can now book a hotel on your mobile, turn up, check in on a screen, all without speaking to another human being. Jobs such as receptionist, typist, travel agent, bank cashier, switchboard operator, and data entry clerk have changed, and many no longer exist. Here in the UK, new graduates are finding it difficult to get work, especially in the field in which they studied.

If this trend continues without consideration to the types of work that keep humans well, healthily busy, engaged, hopeful and certainly not bored, we face significant problems.

Right now, the divisions and inequalities around work can clearly be seen. I have friends that have not worked since they had kids because they didn't need the money. Others have to work three jobs just to keep afloat financially. Some have been able to retire at 50 and are now spending their time on cruises or long-haul holidays – "Got to keep busy, Jen… we don't want to be bored." At the same time, I also know many people who will be working beyond 70, as they still have mortgages.

Whatever our personal circumstances, we could all do with finding work that is less boring, more satisfying, more meaningful and, dare I say, more equitable.

One idea is a shorter working week, supported by the New Economics Foundation:

"Shorter working hours without a loss in pay offers a way to tackle symptoms of overwork, providing people with more time to recuperate, participate in democratic process and fulfil caring responsibilities."

New Economics Foundation (2022)

Other benefits of a shorter working week include spreading the available work to more people, thus reducing unemployment, enabling people to care for elderly family members, helping people develop hobbies, interests and wellbeing routines.

In a recent report, the Royal Society for the Arts, Manufactures and Commerce (known as the RSA) discussed the Future of Work and outlined many ways forward. One of these was the Universal Basic Income, which has been advocated by the Green Party for many years. Providing everyone with a basic level of income would enable people to afford basic housing and living expenses so that further earning could enhance living. Another suggestion from the RSA was around creating lifelong learning for all, so that people can upskill, retrain for new jobs etc. Both of these ideas, in theory, could help people create more meaningful, satisfying work.

"Recrafting work" is an approach and a term coined by positive psychologists to help people shape their current work and find new meaning and satisfaction. They propose that work can be re-crafted, or re-shaped, if you like, to help individuals achieve a higher level of meaning, by moving further along the continuum from having a "job" (just earning money to survive), onto building a "career" (one that is chosen and has more direction), and finally, reaching one's "calling", whatever than might mean.

Seligman's process for Recrafting Work involves: 1) identifying your signature strengths; 2) choosing work that lets you use your strengths every day; 3) re-crafting your present work to use your signature strengths more; 4) making room for other employees to also re-craft their work (Seligman, 2002). Gordon Parry also noted the importance of ongoing support or coaching to build, enhance and sustain hope. This would include clarifying goals, identifying numerous pathways to attainment, summoning energy to maintain pursuit, and reframing insurmountable obstacles into challenges to be overcome (Parry, 2006).

As I write this section about work, I feel I am in danger of sounding like a fantasist or completely out of touch with the realities of daily life. Please know that if viewed in isolation, these ideas are unlikely to work well. To move from having a job just to survive, towards more meaningful work, it would help to have a basic level of income for all, so that there was more freedom and security to change or retrain. A shorter working week needs to happen without a reduction in income otherwise few would opt for it, or it would have to be mandatory, so that the temptation to overwork or do overtime wasn't possible - this only perpetuates the problems. In terms of recrafting work, unfortunately, coaching or support of this type is rarely available and often only for those high up in organisations. Some people craft their own work by working in the "gig" economy. For some, this is a necessity, but for others, it's a choice as they search for more satisfying, flexible work. However, it can be tough in the "gig" economy, with no certainty or safety net.

Less boring ways to age

Perhaps I am a little odd, but as my friends and I get older, it would seem that I am not as odd as I thought. For over 25 years, I worked with older people in hospitals, care homes, and their own homes, and saw many unpleasant situations. Not abuse per se, but isolation, loneliness, lack of activity, and ultimately, boredom. It is often worse when people are taken out of their own environment, which at least might have memories, purposeful routines, and other things to do. Basic needs such as food, hygiene and safety are met, but it's so hard to maintain a meaningful, full, and sociable life with our current practice of isolating older people at home or in one room at a residential or nursing home.

These experiences called me to consider how I would like to live as I get older, so my later years are not lonely and boring. It's fairly unlikely I will have the money for round the world cruises or for a swanky care home with its own cinema, and frankly, even expensive care homes are not always that great.

What could we do differently that might be better? How could we organise our older age in ways that provide wellbeing, care, companionship, and ultimately fend off boredom in the final years of our life?

Communal living, which makes sense on many levels, needs to be transformed, and ideas have surfaced that could work. These might not suit everyone, but embracing a menu of different options that include some of the following would be a lot less boring.

- Older people with a spare room, letting a student or young person live with them for free in return for providing some care, support and company.

- People with big gardens they can't manage could let others who don't have a garden look after it or even grow food.

- How about renting a spare room in someone's home and using it as a studio/office in exchange for providing support of some kind?

- Groups of older friends could combine all or part of their estate and live in a large house together. They could have live-in carers, but whilst they are still able, could cook communally, socialise, have card nights, parties, games nights, film nights, etc. (This is what I plan to do and I have my comrades gathering as we speak.)

- As adults, if we worked a shorter week, we could all contribute a day or two to our local community in terms of caring for older or vulnerable people, reducing the need for a large social care force.

- Residential care homes could be combined with nurseries so that both younger and older people get care and support whilst enjoying each other's company (take a look at Channel 4's programme "Old People's Home for 4 Year Olds").

- What if working later in life was encouraged, as it provides structure, identity, purpose, and company? Some people don't want to retire at 60-67 and would happily work until 75 or older.

- What about "paying" into a care swap scheme, so that you help a local person with their care when you are in your 40s-60s for a few hours a week, and then received that back from someone else, later in your life if you need it?

- What about other skills swapped for care with "older" people tutoring younger people in return for help with housework, shopping, or gardening.

These ideas may sound whacky, but they could work if some barriers were removed, some policies changed, and cultural norms shifted.

Boredom and the big stuff

"Business has helped us to be warm, safe and distracted. It has been markedly indifferent to our flourishing."

The School of Life (2017, p 52)

The economy and a rethink of capitalism

Discontent, including feelings of boredom, not feeling good enough, periods of misunderstood melancholy, and low mood, all feed capitalism. Don't get me wrong, discontent is not all bad – it can fuel social change, innovation, and creativity, but with the good that it might bring, it is unhelpful too. Think about the rise of the smartphone. It wasn't good enough for us to have a basic mobile phone that we kept for six, seven, eight years. Many people now replace their resource-guzzling devices every couple of years. And we don't just have a phone; we might also have a smart watch and a tablet. Did we get bored with our existing phone, crave novelty, feel discontent that our phone won't function like "everyone else's does", or just want to distract ourselves with a new toy?

Supporters of capitalism, and we are all supporting capitalism, must realise that if society was happy and content, capitalism would be in big trouble. Think of all the industries that would struggle to exist if we all felt pretty enough, thin enough, happy enough, and fulfilled enough. Would we need such a massive beauty industry, a booming diet industry, or thousands of self-help books?

Critics of alternative approaches to traditional capitalism often say that if wealth was distributed and the aims of capitalism were shifted away from accumulation and constant growth, that the economic system would lack movement and die. This critique is simplistic and shortsighted, but exploring it fully is way beyond the scope of this book. Suffice to say there are many possible alternatives to our current capitalist system, which don't rely on uncapped, unsustainable growth, environmental damage, and massive inequality. Let's also note that affluence (wealth) is not the predictor of wellbeing and good health that we once assumed (Kahneman & Deaton, 2010). Before I rant for (p)ages, I hope it has been clear from our discussions so far that the economy, the environment and our problem with boredom are inextricably linked. As human "doings", we could change our relationship to boredom, and in doing so, open possibilities for a different type of economy, one that focusses on the planet and its inhabitants flourishing.

"A good future may not depend on not minimising consumer capitalism but radically extending its reach and depth."

The School of Life (2017, p 49)

If human activity creates economy, why not invest in life-enhancing, regenerative activities, that promote a dynamic equilibrium in our economy. Here there would energy and movement, but not endless growth and accumulation of wealth at the expense of the environment and our wellbeing?

- Economic activities that foster wellbeing and social connection, instead of making us ill, burnt-out and isolated.
- Economic activities that regenerate, rebuild, re-create, and protect, instead of depleting and destroying resources.
- Shift the production focus away from "new", disposable, convenience goods, towards cherishing, renewing and recrafting what we already have. This

could provide just as much work – the industry focus would just be aligned differently.

- Economic activities that value individual output rather than mass productivity.
- Activities that are valued for being slow, nurturing, and caring (by this, I mean really valuing what gives us good feelings, such as joy, contentment, quality of experience; I'm thinking massages, original art, live music).

We need to **divest** in the "attention" economy, which focusses on distracting us with disposable, mass-produced goods, and **invest** in a meaningful, wellbeing-focussed economy.

Meaning as new currency

It feels like we have been yearning for this shift for some time. In recent years, there has been a massive increase in people cycling, wild swimming, baking, sewing, gardening and growing, dancing and singing. Perhaps TV shows such as "The Great British Bake Off", "The Sewing Bee", "The Choir" and "Sky Artist of the Year" (!) have all helped. Equipment and resources are more easily available. Shops such as Hobbycraft have sprung up, and of course, we can now easily order materials online with them arriving the next day. You can pretty much learn anything from YouTube, or for more formal learning, there are thousands of free or low-cost online courses. Creative writing has boomed with people finding power and freedom in self-publishing. In the US, there was a 264% increase in self-published books from 2013-2018 (Piersanti, 2020). Music festivals and other types of festivals have boomed in the last 30 years, providing a mix of fresh air, music, company, and camping, and despite appalling toilets, people flock to them.

People really seem to want to do stuff every day that is active, sensory-stimulating, memory-making, nurturing, tasty, fun, and sociable. Events and activities that are meaningful to us don't tend to be boring, and we are more self-motivated to initiate and engage with them.

Choosing meaningful, mindful doing really can be a win-win-win all round.

The idea of "meaning" as potent currency, as a form of value, is gaining ground. Our consumer habits are changing, with a desire to buy local, crafted products, goods with less air miles attached, and buying from ethical companies paying fair wages. Businesses with more meaningful outcomes in mind tend to play the long game, as they don't just focus on immediate profit. Investors are slow to change, but are putting more of their money in companies with social, ethical, and environmental aims and governance.

There has also been a massive growth in people giving experiences as gifts instead of a physical present. These gift experiences such as sending a friend for an afternoon tea, a spa day or a gin-making workshop are clear indications of the importance of meaning and memory-making, which you don't get from monogrammed napkins or a mass-produced candle.

The growth in a more meaningful economy goes beyond what we do and buy. In recent years, there has been huge expansion in the self-development industry, be it books, services, classes, life coaching, or therapy. Man's search for meaning is really ramping up, and I hope Victor Frankl would be slightly proud of us...

The last word(s)

This last section originally started with a desperate plea to tackle climate change, but I decided this was the wrong way to go. One, because I think we have switched off and become "bored" with climate change; two, because focussing on the problem itself seems to be making it worse somehow; and three, because you decided to buy a book about boredom, and no one wants to feel let down during the last pages of a book.

It seems clear that creating more meaning in our daily lives is key to tackling boredom and to giving us all a better quality of life. However, in trying to make that meaning, we risk worsening the climate crisis if we are not careful, especially if we do things like the "life-changing around the world trip" or the "wardrobe makeover" or the "house renovations".

It might feel like a "Catch-22" in some ways. If we don't find meaning and purpose, we remain disconnected, weary, isolated, and bored, and are at greater risk of anaesthetising ourselves with food, alcohol, drugs of all kinds, or becoming an activity junkie.

I am an optimist though, albeit a weary one sometimes, and reckon we can tackle boredom, find enjoyment, meaning, connection, wellbeing, belonging, variety, achievement, purpose, and all those delicious things whilst tackling climate change and building a more sustainable future. However, we need imagination, and to let go of some of our long-held and often unhelpful beliefs.

To respond to the lovely Bregman and Manton's (2018) call for a "new utopia", one that is fit for realists, here are some of the things I would include in my utopia.

- What if we were satisfied by a holiday in our own country? What if the beautiful beaches, hills and mountains of the UK could satiate our "dromomania" and provide really good holidays, instead of us saying, "Oh, we are **just** staying in the UK this year…" as if it were some sort of failure and not as good as getting on a plane.

- What if home-cooked meals were seen as a luxury, not a burden, and their production was fun and didn't play into gender stereotypes?

- What if upcycled clothes became as desirable as fast-fashion, and added to the economy and job prospects?

- What if the wellbeing economy was truly valued and that things like having a massage every week or doing lunchtime yoga at work was the norm?

- What if the arts were valued, and having original art in our homes was normal, with artists paid a fair price for their work?

- What if well-paid, part-time work was the norm for the whole of our working life, allowing us more time to care for family members, look after ourselves and have more free time?

- What if we weren't obsessed by home ownership and instead chose to live communally, somehow?

This would give us company, less housework, smaller bills, and all sorts of more interesting ways to live.

- What if schools were smaller, focussed on practical/emotional skills, and were held in different environments such as forests?

I reckon that all sounds much better for us human "doings", the planet we live on, and importantly, much less boring.

Thanks for reading.

References

A Multisensory Room For Fighting Depression? (2019). Retrieved 9 February 2022, from https://www.experia-usa.com/blog/a-multisensory-room-for-fighting-depression/

Abbas, N., Abrar ul Haq, M., Ashiq, U., & Ubaid, S. (2020). Loneliness among elderly widows and its effect on social and mental well-being. Global Social Welfare, 7(3), 215-229.

Abbott, A. (2011). Dementia: a problem for our age. Nature, 475(7355), S2-S4.

Blatherwick, L. (2021). A Practical Self-Help Guide to Managing Comfort Eating. Routledge.

Bregman, R., & Manton, E. (2018). *Utopia for realists: And how we can get there.* Bloomsbury.

Brown, C., Tollefson, N., Dunn, W., Cromwell, R., & Filion, D. (2001). The adult sensory profile: Measuring patterns of sensory processing. The American Journal of Occupational Therapy, 55(1), 75-82.

Bruss, K. (2012). Searching for boredom in ancient Greek rhetoric: Clues in Isocrates. Philosophy & rhetoric, 45(3), 312-334.

Dahlen, E. R., Martin, R. C., Ragan, K., & Kuhlman, M. M. (2004). Boredom proneness in anger and aggression: Effects of impulsiveness and sensation seeking. Personality and Individual Differences, 37(8), 1615-1627.

Danckert, J., & Merrifield, C. (2018). Boredom, sustained attention and the default mode network. Experimental brain research, 236(9), 2507–2518. https://doi.org/10.1007/s00221-016-4617-5

Doehlemann, M., (1991). Boredom. Interpretation of a common phenomenon. Frankfurt am Main: Suhrkamp.

Eastwood, J. D., Frischen, A., Fenske, M. J., & Smilek, D. (2012). The unengaged mind: Defining boredom in terms of attention. Perspectives on Psychological Science, 7(5), 482-495.

Ettema, D., & Smajic, I. (2015). Walking, places and wellbeing. The geographical journal, 181(2), 102-109.

Eysenck, H. J. (1967) The biological basis of personality. Charles C. Thomas. [MZ] (1990) Biological dimensions of personality. Handbook of personality: Theory and research, ed. LA Pervin, 244276.

Farmer, R., & Sundberg, N. D. (1986). Boredom proneness--the development and correlates of a new scale. Journal of personality assessment, 50(1), 4-17.

Foley, R. (2017). Swimming as an accretive practice in healthy blue space. Emotion, Space and Society, 22, 43-51.

Foley, R. A. (2016). Mosaic evolution and the pattern of transitions in the hominin lineage. Philosophical Transactions of the Royal Society B: Biological Sciences, 371(1698), 20150244.

Gallagher, W. (2009). Rapt: Attention and the focused life. Penguin.

Gershuny, J. (2005). Busyness as the badge of honor for the new superordinate working class. Social research, 287-314.

Glackin, O. F., & Beale, J. T. (2018). 'The world is best experienced at 18 mph'. The psychological wellbeing effects of cycling in the countryside: an Interpretative Phenomenological Analysis. Qualitative Research in Sport, Exercise and Health, 10(1), 32-46.

Goodreads. (n.d.). A quote by Ellen Goodman. Goodreads. Retrieved January 28, 2022, from https://bit.ly/3LidLZn

Hansen, B. (2020, November 2). *5 ways reading can change your life (and best practices)*. Cornerstone University. https://www.cornerstone.edu/blog-post/5-ways-reading-can-change-your-life-and-best-practices/

Harari, Y. N. (2014). Sapiens: A brief history of humankind. Random House.

Harvard Health. (2020). Increased well-being: Another reason to try yoga. Retrieved 14 February 2022, from https://www.health.harvard.edu/mind-and-mood/increased-well-being-another-reason-to-try-yoga

Havermans, R. C., Vancleef, L., Kalamatianos, A., & Nederkoorn, C. (2015). Eating and inflicting pain out of boredom. Appetite, 85, 52-57.

Hidaka, B. H. (2012). Depression as a disease of modernity: explanations for increasing prevalence. Journal of affective disorders, 140(3), 205-214.

Hoffman, E. (2017). How to be Bored. Picador

Hunter, A., & Eastwood, J. D. (2018). Does state boredom cause failures of attention? Examining the relations between trait boredom, state boredom, and sustained attention. Experimental Brain Research, 236(9), 2483-2492.

Inayatullah, S., & Milojević, I. (2022). Futures Studies by Sohail Inayatullah and Ivana Milojević. Retrieved 14 February 2022, from https://www.metafuture.org/

Iso-Ahola, S. E., & Crowley, B. D. (1991). Adolescent Substance Abuse and Leisure Boredom. Journal of Leisure Research, 23, 260-271

Janaway, C. (1999). Schopenhauer's pessimism. Royal Institute of Philosophy Supplements, 44, 47-63.

Jepson, A. (2016). Gardening and wellbeing: A view from the ground. In Making and Growing (pp. 147-162). Routledge.

Jola, C., & Calmeiro, L. (2017). The Dancing Queen. The Oxford handbook of dance and wellbeing, 13.

Kabat-Zinn, J. (2017). Lovingkindness meditation. Mindfulness, 8(4), 1117-1121.

Kahneman, D., & Deaton, A. (2010). High income improves evaluation of life but not emotional well-being. Proceedings of the national academy of sciences, 107(38), 16489-16493.

Kirby, A. (2001). BBC News | HEALTH | NHS urged to promote washable nappies. Retrieved 9/2/22 http://news.bbc.co.uk/1/hi/health/1287722.stm#:~:te xt=It%20will%20take%20200%20to,legacy%20to%20y our%20children's%20grandchildren.&text=%22The%2

0production%20of%20disposables%20uses,renewable%20resources%20than%20real%20nappies.

Lee, F. K., & Zelman, D. C. (2019). Boredom proneness as a predictor of depression, anxiety and stress: The moderating effects of dispositional mindfulness. Personality and Individual Differences, 146, 68-75.

LePera, N. (2011). Relationships between boredom proneness, mindfulness, anxiety, depression, and substance use. The New School Psychology Bulletin, 8(2), 15-25.

Lester, D. (2010). Extraversion and the autonomic nervous system: an alternative to Eysenck's theory. Int. J. Psychol. Res, 409.

Lin, Y., & Westgate, E. (2021). The origins of boredom.

Malcolm, M., Frost, H., & Cowie, J. (2019). Loneliness and social isolation causal association with health-related lifestyle risk in older adults: a systematic review and meta-analysis protocol. Systematic Reviews, 8(1), 1-8.

Marks, N. A., Cordon, C., Aked, J., & Thompson, S. (2008). Five ways to wellbeing. New economics foundation, 1-23.

Martin, M., Sadlo, G., & Stew, G. (2006). The phenomenon of boredom. Qualitative Research in Psychology, 3(3), 193-211.

Maslow, A. H. (2013). *Toward a psychology of being.* Simon and Schuster.

McDonald, S., O'Brien, N., White, M., & Sniehotta, F. F. (2015). Changes in physical activity during the retirement transition: a theory-based, qualitative interview study. International Journal of Behavioral Nutrition and Physical Activity, 12(1), 1-12.

McRobbie, L. (2021). The History of Boredom. Retrieved 30 July 2021, from https://www.smithsonianmag.com/science-nature/the-history-of-boredom-138176427/#:~:text=Boredom's%20Origins,dates%20back%20a%20lot%20further.

Milkman, H. B., & Sunderwirth, S. G. (2009). *Craving for ecstasy and natural highs: A positive approach to mood alteration*. Sage.

Miller, K. (2019). 14 Health Benefits of Practicing Gratitude According to Science. Retrieved 14 February 2022, from https://positivepsychology.com/benefits-of-gratitude/

Moynihan, A. B., Tilburg, W. A. V., Igou, E. R., Wisman, A., Donnelly, A. E., & Mulcaire, J. B. (2015). Eaten up by boredom: consuming food to escape awareness of the bored self. *Frontiers in psychology*, *6*, 369.

New Economics Foundation (2022). A shorter working week. Retrieved 14 February 2022, from https://neweconomics.org/campaigns/shorter-working-week

Nyman, S. R., & Szymczynska, P. (2016). Meaningful activities for improving the wellbeing of people with dementia: beyond mere pleasure to meeting fundamental psychological needs. Perspectives in public health, 136(2), 99-107.

Peters, D. (2016). Our growing fascination with boredom. Retrieved 8 February 2022, from https://www.universityaffairs.ca/features/feature-article/growing-fascination-boredom/

Piersanti, S. (2020). 10 Awful Truths About Publishing. Retrieved 14 February 2022, from https://ideas.bkconnection.com/10-awful-truths-about-publishing

Preskey, N. (2021). This is what a year of monotony has done to your brain. Retrieved 8 February 2022, from https://www.independent.co.uk/life-style/health-and-families/boredom-impact-brain-body-lockdown-b1822898.html

Raffaelli, Q., Mills, C., & Christoff, K. (2018). The knowns and unknowns of boredom: a review of the literature. Experimental brain research, 236(9), 2451-2462.

Raleigh, V. (2021). What is happening to life expectancy in England?. Retrieved 9 February 2022, from https://www.kingsfund.org.uk/publications/whats-happening-life-expectancy-england?gclid=Cj0KCQiAoY-PBhCNARIsABcz772C_IJwC1NKEtp6nUev-tUAveofmiX38STEvWDDRyMHNS7-8JGy6NoaAvieEALw_wcB

Rubia, K., Alegría, A. A., & Brinson, H. (2014). Brain abnormalities in attention-deficit hyperactivity disorder: a review. Rev Neurol, 58(Suppl 1), S3-16.

Runco, M. A. (2015). Meta-creativity: Being creative about creativity. Creativity Research Journal, 27(3), 295-298.

Rupp, D. E., & Vodanovich, S. J. (1997). The role of boredom proneness in self-reported anger and aggression. Journal of Social Behavior & Personality, 12(4), 925–936

Schoen, S. A., Ferrari, V., & Spielmann, V. (2021). A Trampoline Exercise Group: Feasibility, Implementation, and Outcomes. The American Journal of Occupational Therapy, 75(Supplement_2), 7512520395p1-7512520395p1.

Selye, H. (1976). Stress without distress. In Psychopathology of human adaptation (pp. 137-146). Springer, Boston, MA.

Serafini, G., Gonda, X., Canepa, G., Pompili, M., Rihmer, Z., Amore, M., & Engel-Yeger, B. (2017). Extreme sensory processing patterns show a complex association with depression, and impulsivity, alexithymia, and hopelessness. Journal of affective disorders, 210, 249-257.

Svendsen, L. (2005). A philosophy of boredom. Reaktion Books.

The School of Life. (2017). How to Reform Capitalism (p. p52). London.

Toohey, P. (2011). Boredom: A lively history. Yale University Press.

Valtorta, N. K., Moore, D. C., Barron, L., Stow, D., & Hanratty, B. (2018). Older adults' social relationships and health care utilization: A systematic review. American journal of public health, 108(4), e1-e10.

Vingerhoets, A. J., Van Huijgevoort, M., & Van Heck, G. L. (2002). Leisure sickness: a pilot study on its prevalence, phenomenology, and background. Psychotherapy and psychosomatics, 71(6), 311–317. https://doi.org/10.1159/000065992

Waters, M. (2021). Amazon now ships more parcels than FedEx. Retrieved 9 February 2022, from https://www.modernretail.co/platforms/amazon-now-ships-more-parcels-than-fedex/

Westgate, E. C. (2020). Why boredom is interesting. Current Directions in Psychological Science, 29(1), 33-40.

Westgate, E. C., & Wilson, T. D. (2018). Boring thoughts and bored minds: The MAC model of boredom and cognitive engagement. Psychological Review, 125(5), 689.

Wilcock, A. (1993). A theory of the human need for occupation. Journal of Occupational science, 1(1), 17-24.

Women still doing most of the housework despite earning more. (2019). Retrieved 9 February 2022, from https://www.ucl.ac.uk/epidemiology-health-care/news/2019/nov/women-still-doing-most-housework-despite-earning-more

Printed in Great Britain
by Amazon

37469793R00076